Management Spreadsheets®

with

Microsoft® Excel

ICDL Professional®

Conor Jordan

Conor Jordan

This edition published 2022

Copyright © Conor Jordan 2022

E-mail: conorjordan@gmail.com

Web: www.digidiscover.com

ISBN : 978-1-7396547-3-3

International Computer Driving License, ICDL, are all registered Trademarks of ICDL Foundation Limited. The content of this book was created with permission from The ICDL Foundation Ltd.

Microsoft®, Windows®, Word®, Excel®, PowerPoint®, Access® and Outlook® are trademarks of the Microsoft Corporation. Screenshots and names were used with permission from Microsoft.

Conor Jordan is unaffiliated with Microsoft or ICDL Foundation Ltd.

The intent of this manual is to provide a guide for readers to help them understand the advanced spreadsheet techniques and features associated with using Microsoft Excel®.

Conor Jordan does not guarantee readers will pass their respective exams because of reading this book. Its purpose is to enable readers to better understand the application that may or may not help them achieve their desired results in exams.

Revision sections are for practice purposes only and are not official ICDL tests. Sample tests for each module can be downloaded from the ICDL website to prepare students for their exams.

This book aims to give readers a clear understanding of the advanced features of Microsoft Excel. It aims to achieve this by providing a step-by-step guide describing the skills needed to use this application effectively.

Downloading Resources

Resources associated with this book provide the opportunity to practice the techniques outlined. This will save the learner time to focus on the practical exercises. Visit www.digidiscover.com/downloads and click on the manual you are using.

Files should be saved in an ICDL Professional folder in 'Documents' on your computer.

Introduction

ICDL Professional is a series of digital skills modules developed to improve learners' employment prospects, capability, and competency and build on their existing knowledge. Subjects covered include advanced word processing, management spreadsheets, financial spreadsheets, advanced presentation, and advanced database. Learners can add to their learner profile using any combination of completed modules tailored to suit their workplace requirements.

The advanced modules, formally known as Advanced ECDL, which covered Microsoft Word, Excel, PowerPoint, and Access applications, have become part of the ICDL Professional series of computer modules. There are now fifteen separate modules, with a new e-commerce module soon becoming available.

The spreadsheet guidance covered in this book may help readers develop their understanding of advanced Microsoft Excel features and may prepare readers for their Management Spreadsheets exam. Successful completion of this module can be added to their ICDL Professional learner profile.

For this book, it is recommended you have access to Microsoft Excel 2016 or later as many of the core features described and illustrations used to involve the latest Microsoft 365 Excel application using Windows on a PC. Many new additions to Microsoft Excel include cloud-based services such as OneDrive and newly added Ribbon display options. The Tell Me help function, the Smart Lookup feature used for research purposes, and many new chart types such as 3D maps and Histograms were included. Since earlier versions, the Microsoft Excel ribbon has changed with collaboration and sharing tools. For this book, the core components covered in the Management Spreadsheet exam can be used with earlier versions of Microsoft Excel.

When I began learning advanced spreadsheets, I often spent long moments scanning the groups, tabs, ribbons, and different buttons on-screen, searching for the correct function. I was familiar with the software's layout but struggled to use its less obvious features. The practical aspects of the application evaded me, and I became frustrated and disheartened. It was acquiring the skills and knowledge I needed to perform tasks effectively proved to be a long, laborious endeavour.

As I became familiar with its many advanced features, I found a more straightforward way of learning. Understand what I was doing, why it was necessary, and examples of how I might apply it to real-life situations. This is why I have written this book. I hope to share my knowledge with readers that may help them improve their existing skills using Microsoft Excel.

It may seem daunting at first, but learn steps one at a time. If parts prove difficult, take note of it and move on, reviewing it later with a new perspective. I hope you find this book helpful and that you progress towards using Microsoft's other applications, including Word, PowerPoint, and Access.

Microsoft Excel is available for PC and Mac. Many of the practical exercises outlined in this book are for Windows PC users. Mac users may find some of the steps, tools, dialog boxes, and features have different names or are positioned elsewhere on the screen. If you encounter any tools with other names on a Mac, it may require some time to search for them. The basic functionality is the same. It may be displayed on-screen elsewhere.

Microsoft Excel is used to create spreadsheets for budgets, financial forecasting, accounts, calculations for loans, savings, and investments, and presenting information visually using a range of charts, PivotTables, and outlines.

Independent sole traders, entrepreneurs, administrative staff, managers, and retailers are just some of the business users of Microsoft Excel. Advanced spreadsheet skills allow readers to build on their current understanding of the application, enhance their career prospects, and make performing repetitive tasks easier and more efficient.

Students can also benefit from learning advanced spreadsheet techniques. Whether they want to improve their knowledge of budgeting and accounts, performing advanced calculations, summarising and displaying large amounts of numerical data, and limiting input using data validation and auditing, acquiring the necessary skills required to do this is provided in this book.

How to use this book

I have divided the book into seven parts, each one containing a number of easily navigable sections:

Management Spreadsheets will cover:

Section 1 – Formatting. Here, you will learn how to apply conditional formatting to numbers in a spreadsheet; set custom number formats to cells such as date, time, and currency displays; copy and move worksheets; hide and unhide rows, columns, and worksheets; and save worksheets as templates.

Section 2 – Formulae and Functions. This section will explain how you can apply complex formulae to numerical and financial information to perform calculations. You will learn about logical functions that determine whether specific values meet certain criteria, mathematical functions that add values together depending on their amounts, and financial functions that calculate present and future values of a loan.

Section 3 – Charts. This section demonstrates how to apply a range of advanced settings to different charts, including secondary axis, data series, scale of value axis, and data label formatting. These apply to a selection of charts, including bar, column, line, pie, and combo.

Section 4 – Analysis. Spreadsheet analysis covers the creation and modification of PivotTables to summarise information; data tables that perform many calculations using variable amounts; sorting and filtering information contained within tables; and the use of scenarios in financial predictions.

Section 5 – Validating and Auditing. In this section, you will learn how to limit the type of data you can enter into tables using data validation. You will find out how to uncover faults in formulae by tracing precedents, dependents, and errors in a worksheet. You will learn to create, edit, reply to, and delete comments in a worksheet.

Section 6 – Excel Productivity. Increase productivity using spreadsheets by applying names to groups of data and formulae; using Paste Special to copy cell ranges; linking worksheets to external files, websites, and other spreadsheets; and creating automated tasks with macros.

Section 7 – Collaborative Editing. Develop ways of working on projects with others by comparing, editing, reviewing, and merging spreadsheets; applying password protection to cells, worksheets, and workbooks; and showing and hiding formulae in a worksheet.

Contents

Section 1

Formatting

In this section, you will learn:

- Conditional formatting for numerical values

- Custom number formats and their applications

- Saving workbooks as templates

Apply Conditional Formatting

Conditional formatting applies formatting to cells depending on the value of the cells. Suitable formatting applies depending on the rules set for a range of cells. This type of formatting makes viewing values in a spreadsheet easier. Conditional formatting can also apply by using formulas. For instance, using the =average formula will apply formatting to all the cells above or below the average range of cells.

1. Open the workbook **Conditional Formatting**

2. Highlight cells B6:M6

3. On the **Home** tab in the **Styles** group, select **Conditional Formatting**

4. Select **New Rule**

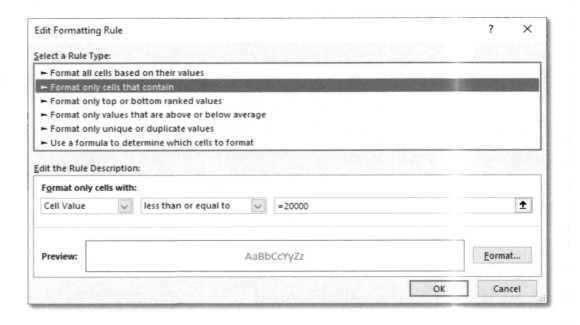

5. Select **Format Only Cells that Contain**

6. Set the **Rule Description** as **Cell Values less than or equal to 20000**

7. Click on the **Format** button

8. Choose a **Red** colour

9. Click **OK**

10. Click **OK** again

11. Formatting applies to any cells with a value less than or equal to €20,000

12. On the **Home** tab in the **Styles** group, select **Conditional Formatting**

13. Select **New Rule**

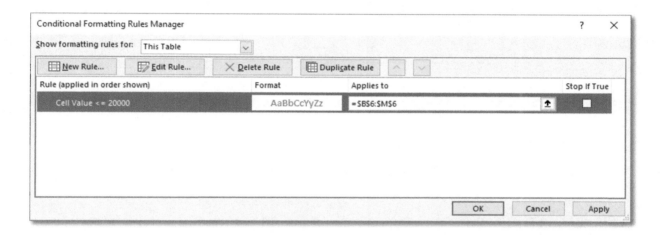

14. Select the rule and click on the **Delete Rule** button

15. Click **OK**

16. You have deleted the rule

17. On the **Home** tab in the **Styles** group, select **Conditional Formatting**

18. Select **New Rule**

19. Choose **Format only top or bottom ranked values**

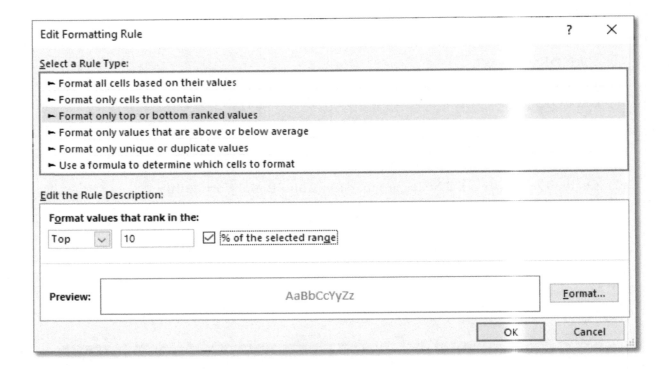

20. Select the **% of the selected range** checkbox

21. Format with **Red Text**

22. Click **OK**

23. The top ten per cent of values appear formatted

24. On the **Home** tab, select **Conditional Formatting** and choose **Manage Rules**

25. Select the **Top 10%** rule and click on **Delete Rule**

26. You have removed the rule from the selected cells

27. Save the worksheet again and close it

Custom Number Formats

Custom number formats apply formatting to cells using text, numerical values, thousand or decimal separators, and time and date formatting. Custom number formats can be applied to selected cells to change the way values appear in cells, e.g. dd/mm/yy will display 14/09/21. Without formatting applied to that cell, the values within the cell would appear as 140921, making it difficult to understand.

d	Day number e.g. 4
dd	Day number with two numbers, e.g. 04
ddd	Day with shortened text, e.g. Mon
dddd	Day with full text, e.g. Monday
m	Month e.g. 6
mm	Month with two numbers, e.g. 06
mmm	Month with shortened text, e.g. Jun
mmmm	Month with full text, e.g. June
h	Hours
#	Displays only digits
0	Displays leading zeros
?	Adds space to either side of the decimal point
,	Thousands separator
.	Decimal separator

1. Open the **Sales Figures** workbook

2. Highlight cells B4:C15

3. On the **Home** tab, in the **Cells** group, click on **Format**, select **Format Cells**

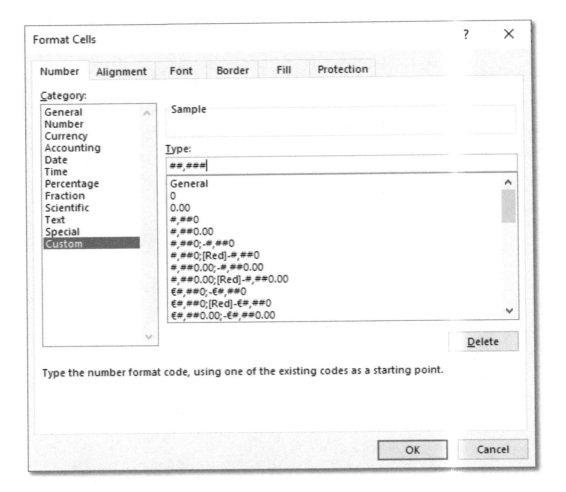

4.   On the **Number** tab, under **Category,** click on **Custom**

5.   In the **Type** box enter ##,###

6.   Click **OK**

7.   The format of the cells will change to thousands

8.   In cell C1, press **Ctrl+;** (Semi-Colon) to enter the current date

9.   Display the **Format Cells** dialog box and click the **Custom** category

10.   Enter **dd/mm/yy** in the **Type** box to format the contents of the cell to a **Date** format

11.   Click **OK**

12.   Save the workbook and close it.

Split Text to Columns

Excel can split this data into columns when you have text in a cell divided by tabs, commas, semicolons, or spaces. For example, if you had a list of days separated by commas contained within one cell in a worksheet, the Split Text to Columns feature can place each day into separate columns.

1. Open a new workbook

2. Type in the following text into cell A2:

    Mon, Tue, Wed, Thu, Fri, Sat, Sun

3. On the **Data** tab in the **Data Tools** group, select **Text to Columns**

4. Choose **Delimited** and click **Next**

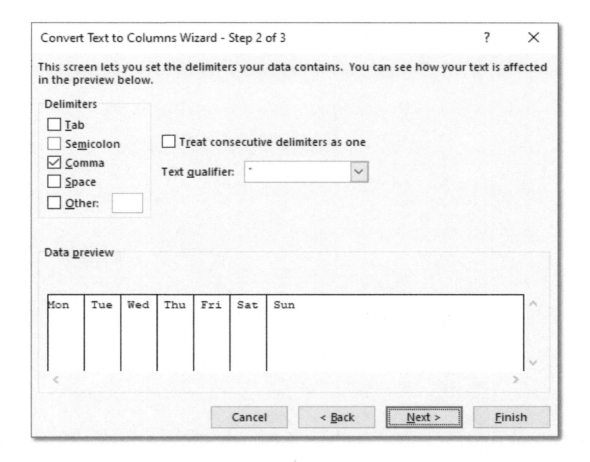

5. Under **Delimiters**, select the **Comma** check box and click **Next**

6. Click **Finish**

7. The text separates into columns

8. Save the workbook as **Columns** and leave it open

Copy & Move Worksheets

Worksheets can be copied and moved to another location in a workbook. The data in the copied or moved worksheet remains intact. A new tab will appear to mark the copied worksheet. You can rename and place it in another location, reordering tabs to organise information in a spreadsheet.

1. Open the **Database Function** workbook

2. Right-click on the **Sheet 1** tab

3. Choose **Move or Copy**

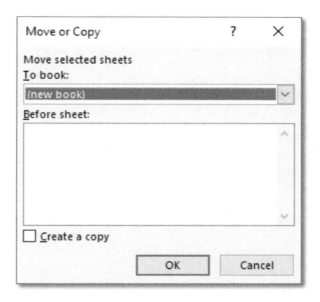

4. Under **To Book:** select **(new book)**

5. Select the **Create a Copy** checkbox to create a copy of the worksheet

6. Click **OK**

7. The worksheet copied to a new workbook

8. Return to the **Database Function** workbook

9. Right-click on the **Sheet 1** tab

10. Choose **Move or Copy**

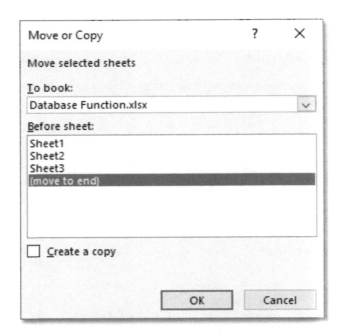

11. For **To Book:** select **Database Function**

12. Under **Before Sheet** select **(move to end)**

13. Do not select the **Create a Copy** checkbox

14. The worksheet moves to the end of the workbook without creating a copy

15. Click **OK**

16. Close both workbooks without saving

Split a Window

Selected columns and rows can remain visible as you scroll through a worksheet using the split a window feature. Applying the split to the top row will ensure the top row remains visible as you move down the worksheet. The same will apply to the first column when a split is applied. The split a window feature helps compare information in large spreadsheets.

1. Open the **Staff List** workbook

2. Select cell B3

3. On the **View** tab in the **Window** group, click on **Split**

4. Use the arrow keys to move down the spreadsheet. The first two rows will remain visible

5. Move back up the worksheet

6. Press the arrow keys to move to the right of the spreadsheet

7. The first column will remain visible on the worksheet

8. Click and drag on the split lines to move them so that the first four columns appear

9. Use the arrow keys to move to the bottom of the spreadsheet

10. The first four columns display on-screen

11. Click on the **Split** button again to remove the split

12. Close the **Staff List** workbook

Hide & Unhide

Columns and rows can be hidden from view while retaining the original data. This data can be revealed again without changing the contents of the cells. This feature can make comparing data within a worksheet easier and is useful when working with large spreadsheets. For example, when working with a large spreadsheet containing a budget, only totals such as total income and total expenses can be shown using the hide and unhide feature.

1. Open the **Staff List** workbook

2. Right-click on column A

3. Choose **Hide**

4. The column retains the hidden data

5. Right-click on the hidden column's location

6. Choose **Unhide**

7. The column displays once more

8. Right-click on row 3

9. Choose **Hide**

10. The hidden row keeps the information intact

11. Right-click at the point of the hidden row

12. Choose **Unhide**

13. Row 3 appears once more

14. Right-click on the **Staff** tab

15. Choose **Hide**

16. The worksheet is no longer in view

17. Right-click on the point of the hidden sheet

18. Choose **Unhide**

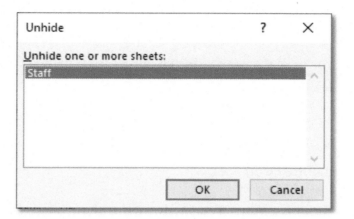

19. The **Unhide** dialog box appears

20. Choose the **Staff** worksheet

21. Click **OK**

22. The **Staff** worksheet appears

23. Save the workbook

Save as a Template

Templates of worksheets and workbooks can be created, designed, and saved for future use. Workbook templates improve efficiency for repeated tasks, such as creating a company invoice or a template for a budget. The formatting, appearance, and formulas within a template will remain the same each time you open the workbook. It is also possible to modify an existing template when adjustments are required.

1. Open the **Staff List** workbook

2. On the **File** tab, select **Save As** and select the **Browse** button

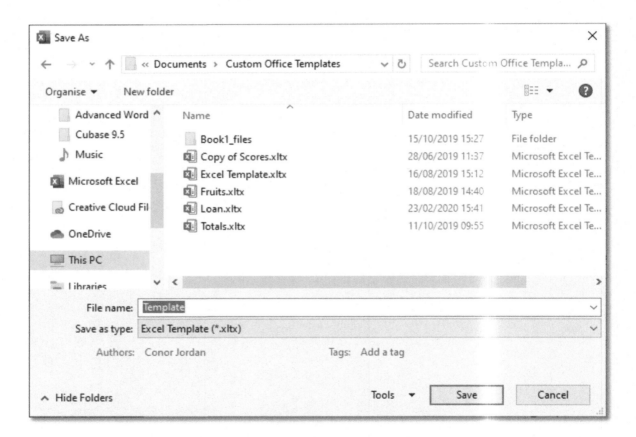

3. In the **File Name** text box, type in **Template**

4. In the **Save As Type** drop-down menu, choose **Excel Template**

5. Click **Save**

6. Close the workbook

7. On the **Excel Home Screen,** select **New**

8. Select **Template** and click on **Create**

9. Edit the **Staff List** title and enter **Employee Records**

10. Highlight the cell range A3:F16

11. Click on the **Delete** button on the keyboard

12. The employee records are removed from the table, leaving a blank table for future use

13. Save the workbook as a template with the same name

14. You have modified the template

15. Close the workbook

Revision - Section 1

1. Open the workbook **Naming Cells**

2. Apply **Conditional Formatting** to the cell range B6:G6 that applies a red coloured font if the value is below €1,800 and a green coloured font if the value is above this amount

3. Apply a **Currency** format with one decimal place to all cells with numerical values

4. Name the worksheet **Income & Expenditure** and copy it to a new workbook

5. Save the workbook as **Finances**

6. Hide rows 4 & 5 in the worksheet and rows 8 to 10

7. Save the workbook as a template named **Finances Template**

8. Close the template

9. Re-open the **Finances Template**

10. **Unhide** all rows

11. Highlight the cell range B4:G12 and delete its contents

12. Save the template with the same name and close it

Summary

Formatting

In this section, you have learned how to:

- Apply conditional formatting rules to numerical information in a worksheet

- Change custom number formats in cells such as date, time, and currency

- Create, modify, and save workbook templates

Section 2

Formulae & Functions

In this section, you will learn:

- Complex formulae and functions for calculations

- Financial formulae to calculate loan repayments and amounts

- Two-level nested functions

Date & Time

Formulas covered here calculate current and existing dates and times in a spreadsheet. For instance, the **=today()** formula displays today's date. The time and date can then be updated whenever you want to use a template without manually entering the date or time. The **=now()** formula displays the current date and time in a selected cell in a worksheet.

1. Open a blank workbook

2. In cell B2, enter **=today()**

3. This enters today's date

4. In cell B3, enter **=now()**

5. This formula enters the current date & time

6. In cell B4, enter **=day(B2)**

7. This formula enters the day value of the selected cell

8. In cell B5, enter **=month(B2)**

9. This formula enters the month value of the selected cell

10. In cell B6, enter **=year(B2)**

11. This formula enters the year value of the selected cell

12. Save the workbook as **Date & Time**

Logical Functions

Logical functions such as And, Or & Not determine if the contents of selected cells meet specified criteria. The answer cell will display a true or false statement depending on whether the requirements met are true or false.

For instance, if you want to check whether a calculation is correct in both selected cells, you can use the **And** function to see whether the answer is True depending on the calculation performed. The **Or** function specifies whether two conditions appear in either one cell or another selected cell. The **Not** function determines whether a calculation is not meeting specific requirements.

1. Open the workbook **Logical functions**

2. Select cell D4

3. On the **Formulas** tab, select **Logical**

4. Select **AND**

5. Enter A4>42000 for **Logical1**

6. Enter C4>2500 for **Logical2**

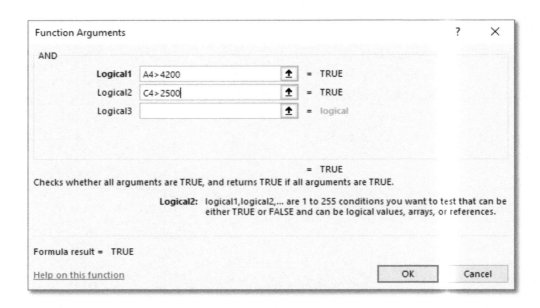

© Conor Jordan 2022

7. The calculation will find out whether sales are greater than €42,000 **AND** net profit is greater than €2,500

8. It produces a **True** result if **Both** conditions satisfy the criteria

9. Click **OK**

10. A true value appears in the answer cell

11. Select cell **D5**

12. On the **Formulas** tab, select **Logical**

13. Select **OR**

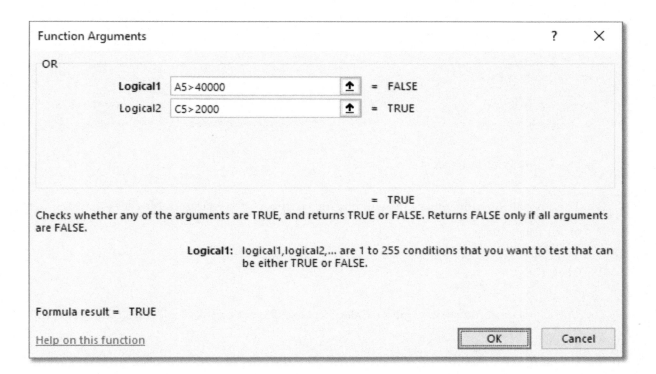

14. Enter A5>40000 for **Logical1**

15. Enter C5>2000 for **Logical2**

16. The calculation finds out whether sales are greater than €40,000 **OR** net profit is greater than €2,000

17. It produces a **True** value if **One** of the conditions satisfies the criteria

18. Click **OK**

19. The calculation produces a **True** result meaning the calculation meets the criteria

20. Select cell D6

21. On the **Formulas** tab, select **Logical**

22. Select **NOT**

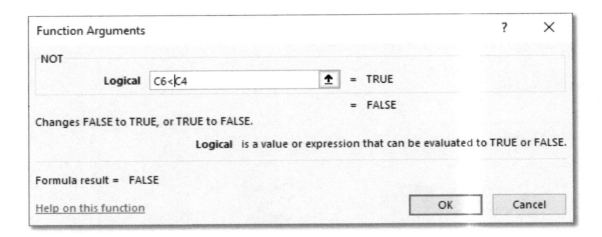

23. For **Logical** enter C6<C4

24. The logical function finds out whether the net profit for March is **Not** less than the net profit for January

25. Click **OK**

26. The calculation returns a value of **False** because the net profit was less than the net profit in cell C4

27. Save the workbook and close it

Mathematical Functions

One mathematical function rounds a number down to the nearest decimal place or zero (**RoundDown**), e.g. €20.34 can be round down to €20.30. Another mathematical function rounds numbers up to the nearest decimal place or zero (**RoundUp**), e.g. €345.86 can be round up to €345.90. Another function adds the values of cells if they meet specific criteria (**Sumif**). For instance, in a list of products in a table, only the products that are above €20 are added together. Products below €20 can also be added from the list using a Sumif function.

1. Open the **Mathematical Functions** workbook

2. Select cell D4

3. On the **Formulas** tab, select **Math & Trig**

4. Choose **RoundDown** from the list of formulas

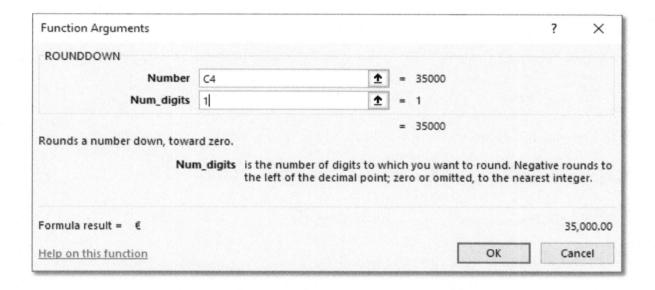

5. Enter C4 for the **Number** textbox and 1 for **Num_digits**

6. The RoundDown function rounds down the numbers to one decimal place

7. Click **OK**

8. Use the **Fill Handle** to copy the formula to D15

9. Select cell E4

10. On the **Formulas** tab, select **Math & Trig**

11. Choose **RoundUp** from the list of formulas

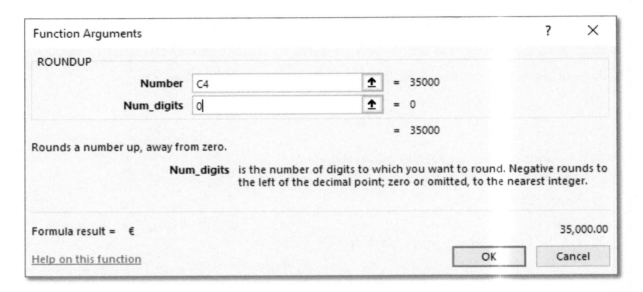

12. Enter C4 for the **Number** textbox and 0 for the **Num_digits** textbox

13. The currency figure rounds up to the nearest whole number

14. Click on **OK**

15. Use the **Fill Handle** to copy the formula to E15

16. Select cell F4

17. On the **Formulas** tab, select **Math & Trig**

18. Choose Sumif from the list of formulas

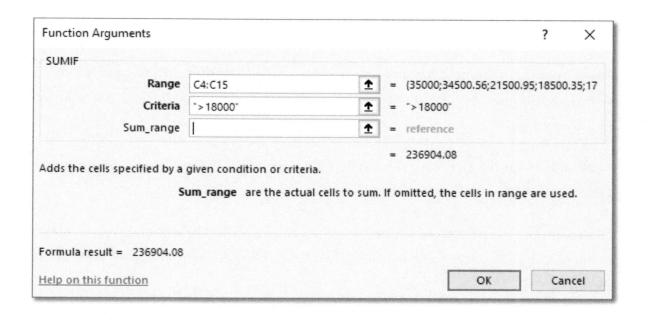

19. Select cells C4:C15 for the **Range** textbox

20. Enter >18000 for the **Criteria** textbox

21. Click **OK**

22. The Sumif formula calculates the total amount of savings for each month for amounts greater than €18,000

23. Save the workbook and close it

Statistical Functions

Statistical functions perform calculations based on set rules. **Countif** is used to count a range of selected cells that meet specified criteria. For instance, only weekly totals above €2,500 count in a sales worksheet.

CountBlank counts the number of blank cells in a range of cells. The formula counts the number of cells that do not contain a value.

Rank.Eq displays the position of a selected cell in a range of cells. For instance, you can use the Rank.Eq function if you want to find the fourth bestselling product out of a range of products sold in a store.

Countif

1. Open the **Statistical** workbook

2. Select cell B16

3. On the **Formulas** tab, select **More Functions** then **Statistical**

4. Select **Countif**

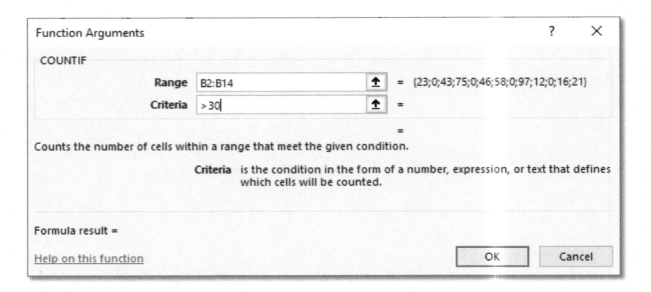

5. Select the **Range** B2:B14

6. Enter the **Criteria** as >30

7. The formula will **Count** the savings for each person **If** the amount is greater than €30

8. Click **OK**

9. The formula counts all the savings amounts that were more than €30

10. Save the workbook and leave it open

CountBlank

1. Open the **Statistical** workbook

2. Select cell B17

3. On the **Formulas** tab, select **More Functions** then **Statistical**

4. Select **CountBlank**

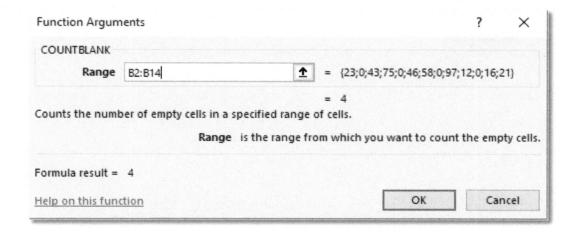

5. The formula **Counts** all the **Blank** cells for people who do not have a savings amount

6. Select the textbox **Range** and highlight cells B2:B14

7. The formula calculates the number of people without a savings amount

8. Click **OK** and leave the workbook open

Rank.Eq

1. With the **Statistical** workbook open, select cell B18

2. On the **Formulas** tab, select **More Functions** then **Statistical**

3. Select **Rank.Eq**

4. In the **Number** text box, choose cell B7

5. In the **Ref** text box, select the range B2:B14

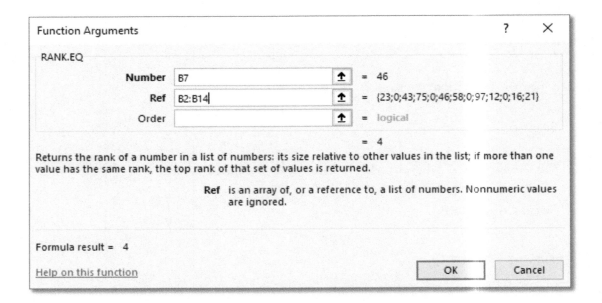

6. The formula finds the **Rank** of Henry's saving amount out of all the amounts saved by each person

7. Click **OK**

8. The formula calculates Henry's saving amount as the fourth highest in the table

9. Save the **Statistical** workbook and close it

Text Functions

Text functions can extract text from selected cells, neaten text in cells and bring together text from separate cells.

The function **Left** extracts the left part of the text in a cell depending on the number of characters the user specifies. For instance, if there is a list of products with product numbers, e.g. 465-NHR-836, the left part of the cell is copied to another cell.

The **Right** function extracts text in the right part of a cell depending on the input. The user can copy the 836 part of the product number into a cell from the example above.

The **Mid** function extracts a set number of characters from the middle of a cell. It displays the NHR part from the example above.

Each function makes extracting data from a large spreadsheet easier and more efficient, e.g. in a large wholesale company, these functions can select only products originating from a particular country and organise this data in a separate worksheet.

1. Open the workbook **Text Functions**

2. Select cell C4

3. On the **Formulas** tab, choose **Text**

4. Select **Left**

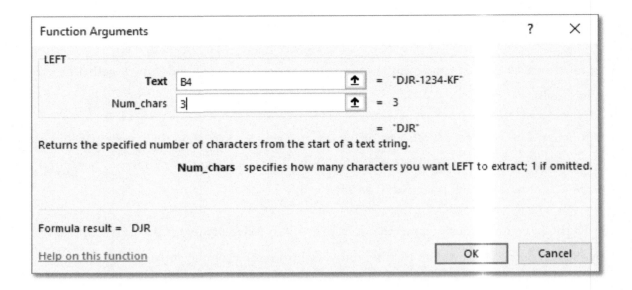

Function Arguments   ?   ✕

LEFT

        Text   B4   ↑ = "DJR-1234-KF"

Num_chars 3   ↑ = 3

                                               = "DJR"

Returns the specified number of characters from the start of a text string.

          Num_chars specifies how many characters you want LEFT to extract; 1 if omitted.

Formula result =   DJR

Help on this function   OK   Cancel

5. Enter B4 for the **Text** textbox

6. For **Num_chars,** type in 3

7. The formula extracts the first three characters from the **Product Reference Numbers**

8. Click **OK**

9. Use the fill handle to copy the formula for each product

10. Select cell D4

11. On the **Formulas** tab, choose **Text**

12. Select **Mid**

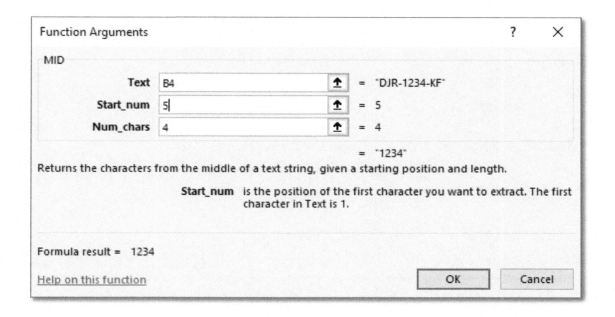

13. In the **Text** textbox, select cell B4

14. For **Start_num,** enter 5

15. For **Num_chars,** type in 4

16. The first four characters appear, starting at the fifth character from the product reference numbers

17. Click **OK**

18. Use the fill handle to copy the formula for all product reference numbers

19. Select cell **E4**

20. On the **Formulas** tab, choose **Text**

21. Select **Right**

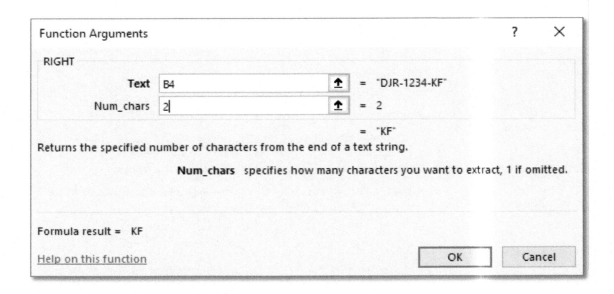

22. Select cell **B4** for the **Text** textbox

23. Type in **2** for the **Num_chars**

24. Click **OK**

25. The function displays the two right characters for the product reference number

26. Use the fill handle to copy the formula for all product reference numbers

27. Save the worksheet as **Products** and keep it open

Trim

The Trim function removes the spaces between text within a cell. The function displays text clearly in a cell and can neaten a range of cells in a worksheet. This function is useful when data is entered into a worksheet incorrectly.

1. With the **Products** workbook open, select cell C9

2. On the **Formulas** tab, choose **Text**

3. Select **Trim**

4. In the **Trim** textbox, select cell A9

5. Click **OK**

6. The function removes unnecessary spaces between the first name and surname of Stephen Hughes

7. Save the workbook and leave it open

Concatenate

This function takes several separate cells containing text and joins them together in another cell. The **Concatenate** function may be applied to a worksheet when you have a list of contact details and want each contact's first name and surname to appear in a single cell.

1. With the **Products** workbook open, select cell D10

2. On the **Formulas** tab, choose **Text**

3. Select **Concat**

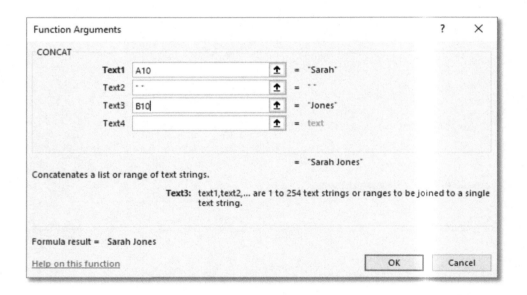

4. In the **Text1** textbox, select A10

5. In the **Text2** textbox, type in""

6. In the **Text3** textbox, select B10

7. The function joins the first name and surname of Sarah Jones in the answer cell

8. Click **OK**

9. The answer cell now displays the Product Manager's name

10. Save the workbook and close it

Financial Functions

Financial functions calculate savings, loan value, and repayments on a loan. These functions can estimate the amount of money an investment will produce, calculate the monthly or annual value of a loan, and the total amount needed to repay a loan.

- Pmt Calculates regular payments required to pay off a loan over a set period

- Pv (Present Value) Calculates the present loan value

- Fv (Future Value) Calculates the final total value of savings

PMT

This function calculates the monthly cost of a loan. It estimates how much you will expect to pay on a loan per month. The calculation includes the interest rate, loan term in months, and loan amount.

1. Open the **Financial Functions** workbook and display the **Monthly Repayments** tab

2. Select cell B5

3. On the **Formulas** tab, choose **Financial**

4. Select **PMT**

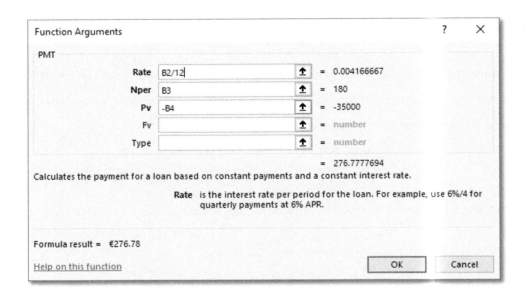

5. In the **Rate** textbox, enter B2/12 to get the **Monthly Rate (Interest Rate)**

6. In the **Nper** textbox, enter B3 **(Total number of monthly payments)**

7. In the **Pv** textbox, enter -B4 **(Value of current loan)**

8. Click **OK**

9. Save the workbook and leave it open

PV

The PV formula calculates the present value of a loan. It determines what the loan is currently worth. The calculation includes the annual rate of the loan, the number of payments, and the monthly repayments amount.

1. With the **Financial Functions** workbook open, display the **PV** worksheet

2. Select cell B6

3. On the **Formulas** tab, choose **Financial**

4. Select **PV**

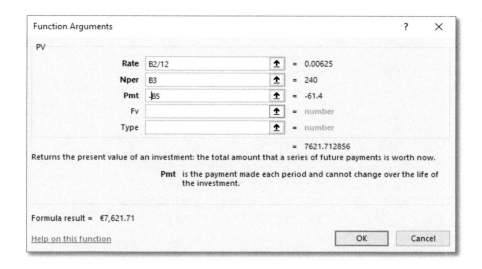

5. In the **Rate** textbox, enter B2/12 to get the monthly interest rate

6. In the **Nper** textbox, type in B3

7. In the **Pmt** textbox, type in -B5

8. The formula calculates the **Present Value** of an investment. It calculates the total amount future payments are worth

9. Click **OK**

10. Save the workbook and leave it open

FV

The FV financial function calculates the future value of savings. It considers the annual rate of a loan, the number of payments, and the monthly repayment amount on a loan. The function calculates the value of a savings account when the savings period ends.

1. Open the **Financial Functions** workbook

2. Display the **FV** worksheet

3. Select cell B6

4. On the **Formulas** tab, choose **Financial**

5. Select **FV**

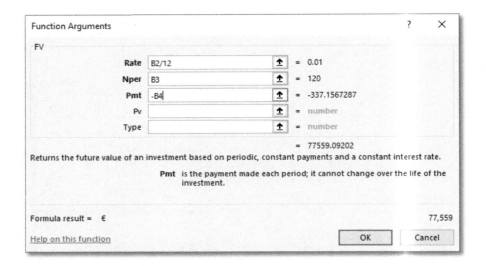

6. In the **Rate** textbox, type in B2/12

7. In the **Nper** textbox, select B3

8. In the **Pmt** textbox, type in -B4

9. It finds the future value of an investment based on regular payments at the same interest rate

10. Click **OK** and save the workbook as **Calculated**

LookUp Functions

LookUp functions search and retrieve information from a table. There is a **VLookUp** function to lookup values in a vertical table. There is also an **HLookUp** function used to lookup values in a horizontal table. These functions include the lookup value, the table array, and the column or row number.

VLookUp

1. Open the **Lookup** workbook and select cell C12

2. On the **Formulas** tab, choose **Lookup & Reference**

3. Select **VLookUp**

4. The formula finds records in a vertical table of data

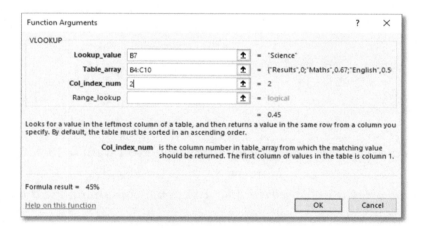

5. In the **Lookup_value** type in B7 **(the value you want to look up)**

6. In the **Table_array** text box select cells B4:C10 **(the table containing the data)**

7. In the **Col_index_num** type in 2 **(the number of the column)**

8. The result displays the record in the vertical table that corresponds to the value searched for

9. Click **OK** and save the document

HLookUp

1. Open the **Lookup** workbook

2. Select cell **C13** as the answer cell

3. On the **Formulas** tab, select **Lookup & Reference**

4. Select **HLookUp**

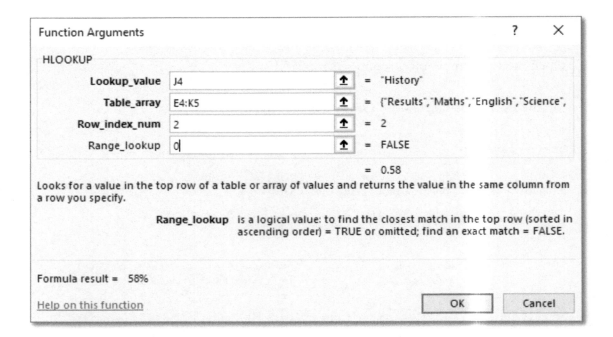

5. In the **Lookup_value** textbox, type in J4 **(the value you want to look up)**

6. In the **Table_array** textbox, select E4:K5 **(the table containing the data)**

7. In the **Row_index_num**, type in 2 **(the row number)**

8. In the **Range_lookup** textbox, type in 0

9. Click **OK**

10. The formula displays the record in the horizontal table that corresponds to the value searched for

11. Save the workbook and close it

Database Functions

Database functions perform calculations in a table of data based on set criteria. **Dsum** adds numbers together in a table of data that includes a range of cells (the criteria), **Dmin** finds the minimum value in a table, **Dmax** finds the maximum value in a table, **Dcount** counts the number of values, and **Daverage** calculates the average out of a table of values. A database in a worksheet is a range of cells that contain numerical information. It can be a table in a worksheet that includes headers. You can set the criteria by selecting the range of cells in a table.

Dsum

1. This function adds numbers in a database depending on specified criteria

2. Open the **Database Function** workbook

3. Select the answer cell B12

4. On the **Formula** tab in the **Function Library,** select **Insert Function**

5. Select the **Database** category

6. Click on **Dsum**

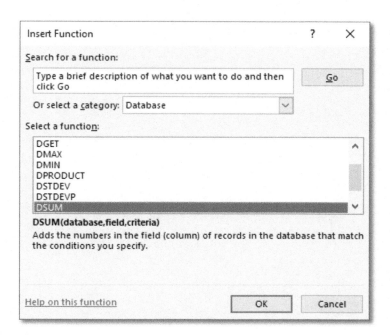

7. Click **OK**

8. Select the cell range A3:E10 for **Database**

9. For the **Field** textbox, select D3

10. For the **Criteria** textbox, select D4:D10

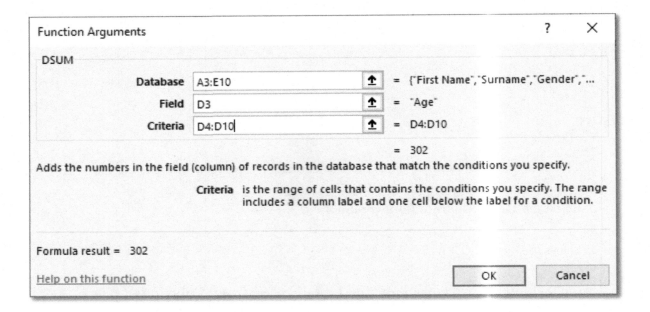

11. Click **OK**

12. The formula adds together the ages of people in the table of data

13. Save the workbook and leave it open

DMIN

The Dmin function finds the minimum value out of a selected range of cells depending on specified criteria. It finds the lowest value from a large selection of cells in a database.

1. Open the **Database Functions** workbook

2. Select cell B13

3. On the **Formula** tab, select **Insert Function**

4. Type in **Dmin** for the search textbox

5. Choose **Dmin**

6. Click **OK**

7. Enter the following information into each textbox:

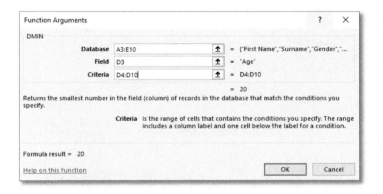

8. Select the range of cells A3:E10 **(Database)**

9. Select the heading of the column cell D3 **(Field)**

10. Select the range of cells D4:D10 **(Criteria)**

11. Click **OK**

12. The function finds and displays the lowest age out of the people in the table

13. Save the workbook and leave it open

DMAX

The Dmax function finds the maximum value out of a range of selected cells in a database. The result depends on criteria specified in the function, e.g. find the maximum value in a range based on specific values.

1. Open the **Database Functions** workbook

2. Select cell B14 as the answer cell

3. On the **Formula** tab, select **Insert Function**

4. Choose **Dmax**

5. Click **OK**

6. Enter the following information into each textbox:

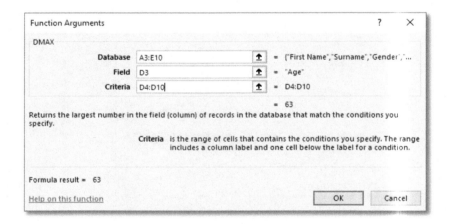

7. Enter A3:E10 for the **Database** textbox

8. Enter D3 for the **Field** textbox

9. Enter D4:D10 for the **Criteria** textbox

10. The function finds and displays the oldest age out of the records contained within the data table

11. Click **OK** and leave the workbook open

Dcount

This function counts the number of cells depending on specific criteria. For instance, if you want to find the range of cells below a particular number, this function will count all the cells below this specified number.

1. Open the **Database Functions** workbook

2. Select cell B15

3. On the **Formula** tab, select **Insert Function**

4. Choose **Dcount**

5. Click **OK**

6. Enter the following information into each textbox:

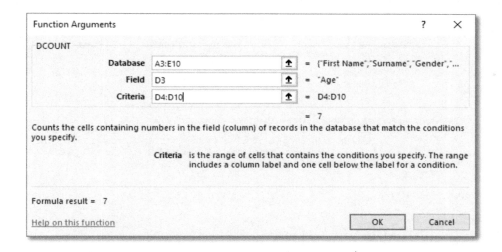

7. For **Database,** enter A3:E10 into the textbox

8. For **Field** enter D3

9. For **Criteria,** enter D4:D10

8. The function counts the number of people in the table

9. Click **OK** and leave the workbook open

Daverage

This function averages the values in a column contained in a table that meets specified conditions, e.g. average all the values above 30 in a list.

1. Open the **Database Functions** workbook

2. Select cell B16

3. On the **Formula** tab, select **Insert Function**

4. Choose **Daverage**

5. Click **OK**

6. Enter the following information into each textbox:

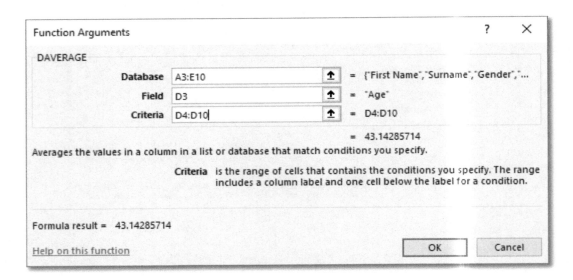

7. In the **Database** textbox, enter A3:E10

8. In the **Field** textbox, enter D3

9. In the **Criteria** textbox, type in D4:D10

10. The function calculates the average age of people in the table

11. Click **OK** and save the workbook as **Database Functions**

Two-Level Nested Function

Functions can be combined where one of the values can be a function itself. It is a function within a function. You can use the **IF** function in this way. For example, **=IF(OR(E2>40,F2<6),20,10)**

The table below calculates **IF** the number of sales is above 40 **OR** the number of days absent is less than 6, and the employee bonus will be €20. If not, the bonus will be €10.

1. Open the **Staff Information** workbook

2. You want to award a **€20 bonus** for staff who had **over 40 sales** or **less than six days absence; if** not, award a **€10 bonus**

3. In cell G2, enter **=IF(OR(E2>40,F2<6),20,10)**

4. Use the fill handle to copy the formula for all staff

5. In cell H2, enter **=IF(AND(C2>35,E2>30),30,10)**

6. The two-level nested function calculates **IF** employees are over 35 **AND** sell more than 30, they receive a €30 bonus; if not, they receive a €10 bonus

7. Save the workbook and close it

3D Reference

This function calculates values on different worksheets. There may be a value in one cell on a single worksheet, and you want to include a value on another worksheet. You can perform this calculation using the 3D reference function.

1. Open the **3D Reference** workbook

Sheet 1

	A	B	C
1	3-D Reference		
2			
3	Sum	25000	
4	Average	30000	
5	Max	54000	
6	Min	24000	
7			
8			

Sheet 2

	A	B	
1	3-D Reference		
2			
3	Sum	43000	
4	Average	54000	
5	Max	15000	
6	Min	75000	
7			

3D Sum

1. On **sheet1** in cell C3, type in **=SUM(B3,**

2. Then move to **sheet2** worksheet and select cell B3

3. Press **Enter**

4. This calculation has added the values in cell B3 on **sheet1** and **sheet2**

3D Average

This function finds the average of cell values on separate worksheets.

1. On the first sheet in cell C4, type in **=AVERAGE(B4,**

2. Then move to **sheet2** and select cell B4

3. Press **Enter**

4. This calculation has averaged the values in cell B4 on **sheet1** and **sheet2**

3D Max

This function finds the maximum value out of selected cells on separate worksheets.

1. On the first sheet in cell C5, type in **=MAX(B5,**

2. Then move to the other worksheet and select cell B5

3. Press **Enter**

4. This calculation has displayed the maximum out of the cell values in B5 on **sheet1** and **sheet2**

3D Min

This function finds the minimum value in a range of cells on separate worksheets.

1. On the first sheet in cell C6, type in **=MIN(B6,**

2. Then move to the other worksheet and select cell B6

3. Press **Enter**

4. This calculation has displayed the minimum value out of cells B6 on **sheet1** and **sheet2**

5. Save the workbook as **3D Referencing**

Mixed Referencing

Mixed Referencing finds out the answer of a formula using two changing amounts. The calculation displays the solution of each formula without the need to type many formulas into a table.

For instance, if you have a variable price of a product and want to find out the discount of that product at different rates, mixed referencing is used to calculate the changing discount at different prices. The fill handle copies the formula across the table.

1. Open the **Mixed Referencing** workbook

2. Place the dollar sign before the first cell reference $B4 and in the middle of the second reference C$3

3. In cell C4, type in: **=$B4*C$3**

4. Use the fill handle to copy the formula horizontally. It calculates the different discount rates at the price of €5

5. Use the fill handle to copy the formula vertically from cell F4, then copy it to cell F7. It will calculate the variable discount of the varying prices

	A	B	C	D	E	F
1						
2			Discount			
3			5%	10%	15%	20%
4	Price	€ 5	€ 0.25	€ 0.50	€ 0.75	€ 1.00
5		€ 10	€ 0.50	€ 1.00	€ 1.50	€ 2.00
6		€ 15	€ 0.75	€ 1.50	€ 2.25	€ 3.00
7		€ 20	€ 1.00	€ 2.00	€ 3.00	€ 4.00
8						

6. Save the workbook as **Discount Calculated** and close it

Revision - Section 2

1. Open the **Functions** workbook

2. Enter today's date using a formula in cell A1

3. Using the **OR** function, check whether the formula answers in cells E3 & E4 are correct and place the answer in cell F3

4. Use the **Fill Handle** to copy to cells F3:F5

5. Use the **RoundDown** function in cell G3 to round the Income cells in column C to the nearest Euro

6. Use the **Fill Handle** to copy to cells G3:G5

7. In cell H3, add only VAT that is above €4,500 in column E

8. Save the workbook as **Revised**

9. Open the **Lodgements** workbook

10. In cell B14, calculate the **Total Amount of Lodgements** above €35

11. In cell D2, combine the first name column with the second name column and copy the formula in the cell range D2:D12

12. In cell B20, calculate the **Monthly Loan Repayments** based on the interest rate, term, and amount provided

13. Save the workbook as **Financial**

14. Open the workbook **Employees List**

15. In cell B6, use a formula to find the employee with an ID of 1006

16. Calculate a bonus of €20 for employees who were absent for less than three days. Include a €10 bonus for employees who are aged 35 and over

17. Use a **Database Function** in cell B18 to find the average age of employees in the cell range A9:G16

18. Save the workbook as **Staff**

Summary

Formulae & Functions

In this section, you have learned how to:

- Apply financial formulae to calculate loan values and repayments

- Use logical functions to return true or false values based on criteria

- Create mathematical functions to perform calculations such as adding values that meet specified criteria

Section 3

Charts

In this section, you will learn:

- Formatting charts including secondary axis and data series

- Changing chart types such as column, bar, pie, and combo

- Repositioning and designing charts for different purposes

Combined Chart

Two data sets can be displayed using a combined line and bar chart or a line and area chart. A combined chart gets its information from two sources and shows them together. The chart often contains different colours for each source, so comparing the data is easier.

1. Open the workbook **Combo Chart**

2. Highlight cells A3:C15

3. On the **Insert** tab, click on **Combo Chart**

4. Select **Clustered Column – Line**

5. Change the **Chart Title** to "Sales Figures"

6. Save the workbook as **Combo Chart**

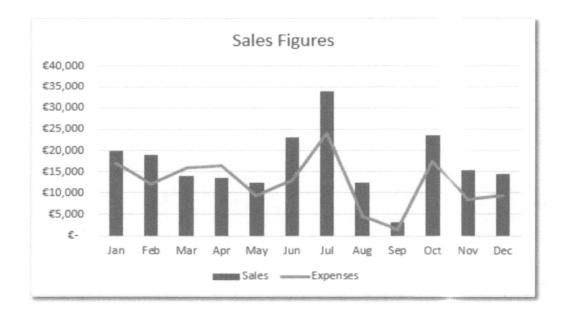

Sparklines

Sparklines are mini charts placed in single cells representing data from a single row. Sparklines display information in chart form in a single cell. They can be copied across a range of cells to visually display the values in a range of cells in chart form.

1. With the **Combo Chart** still open, highlight the range of cells A4:C4

2. On the **Insert** tab in the **Sparklines** group, select **Line**

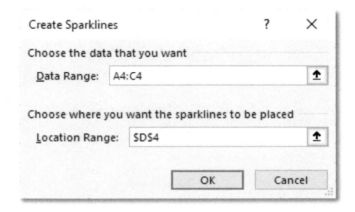

3. In the **Location Range** text box, select cell D4

4. Click **OK**

5. A sparkline appears in cell D4

6. On the **Sparkline** tab, select **Column**

7. Click on the arrow beside **Sparkline Colour** and select a **Red colour**

8. Use the **Fill Handle** to copy the **Sparklines** from D4:D15

9. With cells D4:D15 selected, on the **Sparkline** tab, select **Clear**

10. Save the workbook and leave it open

Add a Secondary Axis to a Chart

The secondary axis displays two or more measured values in a chart. A secondary axis can be added to a chart when a different range of values needs to be displayed. For example, the primary axis may show the sales for a company using bars in a chart, and the secondary axis can display expenses using lines in a chart.

1. With the **Combo Chart** workbook still open, select the chart

2. On the **Chart Design** tab, choose **Change Chart Type** and choose **Combo**

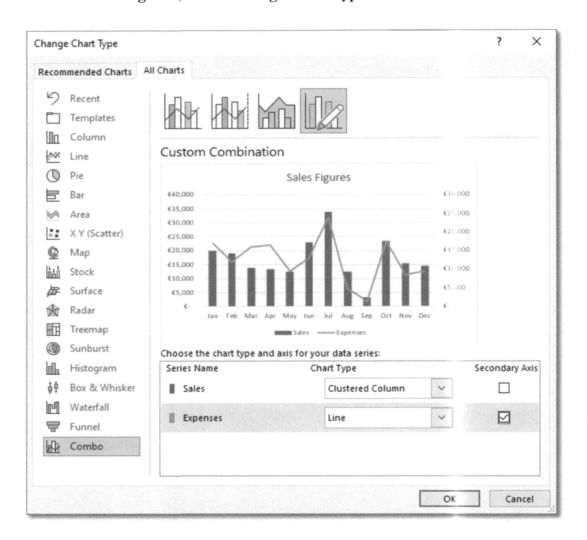

3. For the **Line** chart type displaying expenses, select the **Secondary Axis** checkbox

4. Click **OK**

5. A secondary axis appears to the right of the chart for expenses

6. Save the workbook and leave it open

Changing Chart Type for Data Series

You can display separate information contained in tables depending on the details selected. The chart type for each data series can be changed as many times as is required by choosing different types such as line, bar, column, area, and pie chart. For instance, if you have a combo chart with two data series, one series can be represented using columns and another a line chart.

1. Open the **Combo Chart** workbook

2. Right-click on the **Expenses Line** in the **Combo Chart**

3. Select **Change Series Chart Type**

4. In the **Chart Type** drop-down box, select **Combo,** and under **Area,** choose **Stacked Area**

5. Click **OK**

6. Save the worksheet and leave it open

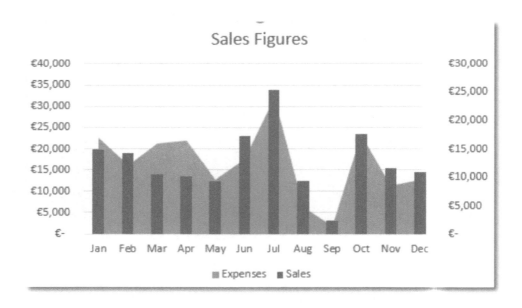

Add/Delete a Data Series

A data series can be added to a chart or removed. Adding and deleting a data series changes the data shown. If you select another data set, this appears in the chart instead. If there is data that is not needed, you can remove it. Depending on what information is required to represent the data clearly, the selected data series can reflect this.

1. Open the **Combo Chart** workbook

2. Right-click on a **Bar** in the chart

3. Select **Delete**

4. Next, add a data series, on the **Chart Design** tab, click on **Select Data**

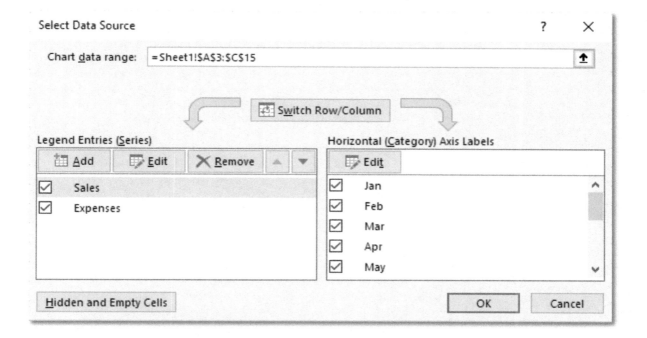

5. In the **Chart Data Range** text box, select the cell range A3:C15

6. Click **OK**

7. The format of the chart has changed to an area data series for sales and expenses

8. Save the workbook and leave it open

Data Label Positioning

Data labels name points on a chart to identify values. You can rearrange data labels depending on the information shown. For example, in a line chart representing expenses, data labels name the values shown in a chart.

1. With the **Combo Chart** workbook still open, click and drag to move the **Chart Title** to the left of the chart

2. Click on the **Legend** beneath the chart

3. Right-click and choose **Format Legend**

4. On the **Format Legend** pane, under **Legend Position**, select **Right**

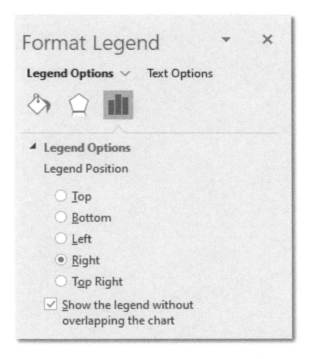

5. On the **Chart Design** tab in the **Charts Layout** group, click on the **Add Chart Element** button and select the arrow beside **Data Labels**

6. Choose **Show**

7. The data labels appear for each **Expenses** data point

8. Click on the **Chart Elements** button and select the arrow beside **Data Labels**

9. Choose **Data Callout**

10. The data labels have now been displayed clearly for each **Expenses** data point

11. Click on the **Chart Elements** button and select the arrow beside **Data Labels**

12. Choose **None**

13. Save the workbook and leave it open

Scale of Value Axis

You can adjust units to display information clearly in a chart. You may want the chart to represent hundreds rather than thousands as it will display the information in the chart more precisely. The minimum and maximum values appear in a chart.

1. Open the **Combo Chart** workbook

2. Right-click on the **Vertical Axis** to the left of the chart and select **Format Axis**

3. In the **Format Axis** pane, under **Bounds,** change the **Minimum** number to display as 1000.0

4. Change the **Maximum** number to display as 80000.0

5. Under **Units**, change the **Major** intervals between units to 1000.0

6. Enter 2000.0 for **Minor Units**

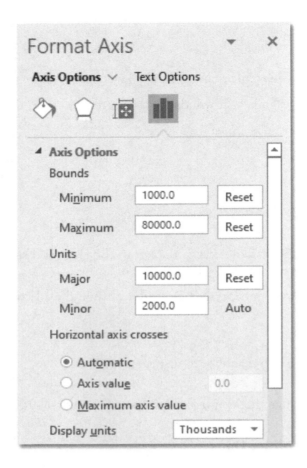

7. For **Display Units,** select **Thousands**

8. Notice the change in the scale of value axis

9. Deselect the **Show display units label on chart**

10. This option removes the **Thousands** label to the left of the vertical axis

11. **Display Units** can show **Hundreds** and **Millions** depending on the range of values in the chart

12. Save the workbook and leave it open

Formatting a Data Series to include an Image

Images can represent chart elements to improve their appearance. For instance, an image can depict the chart background to include more colour. Images can also be placed within columns in a chart to represent data.

1. Open the **Combo Chart** open

2. Adjust the size of the chart by clicking and dragging on the bottom right corner of the chart

3. Select the **Expenses** data series

4. On the **Format Data Series** pane, click on the **Fill & Line** icon

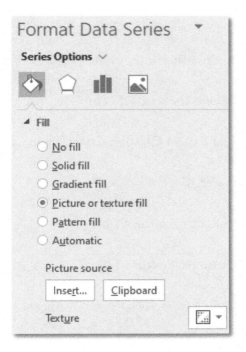

5. Under **Fill**, select **Picture or Texture Fill**

6. Under **Picture Source**, choose **Insert**

7. The **Insert Pictures** box appears

8. Select **From a File**

9. Select the **Computer.png** image contained in the work files folder

10. Click **OK**

11. Right-click on the **Expenses** data series and choose **Change Series Chart Type**

12. Select a **Clustered Column** chart type for the **Sales** data series

13. Click **OK**

14. On the **Format Data Series** pane, select **Stack**

15. The computer images appear stacked on top of each other in the expenses columns

16. On the **Chart Design** tab, select **Change Chart Type**

17. Select **Bar Chart**

18. Click **OK**

19. Click and drag the data series blue lines to include the cell range A3:C9

20. The expenses column shows the stacked computer image

21. On the **Chart Design** tab, select **Change Chart Type**

22. Select **Pie Chart** and click **OK**

23. Select the **January** segment of the **Pie Chart**

24. Under **Fill,** choose **Picture or Texture Fill**

25. On the **Format Data Point** pane, select the **Tile Picture as Texture** checkbox

26. For **Scale X** and **Scale Y,** adjust the percentage to **1%**

27. Change the chart type back to a **Column Chart**

28. On the **Chart Design** tab in the **Chart Styles** group, select **Style 3**

29. Select the **Plot Area** of the chart. The plot area is the chart background.

30. On the **Format Plot Area** pane, select **Picture or Texture Fill**

31. Select the **Tile Picture as Texture** checkbox

32. Adjust the **Scale X** and **Scale Y** to **5%**

33. This option sets the tiled image of the computer as the background to the chart

34. Save the workbook and close it

Revision - Section 3

1. Open the **Sales Figures** workbook

2. Insert a **Clustered Column – Line** chart

3. Using cells A4:C4, insert **Sparklines** in cell D4

4. Change the **Sparklines** to **Columns**

5. Use the **Fill Handle** to copy the **Sparklines** to the range D4:D15

6. Add a **Secondary Axis** to the chart

7. Change the **Loss** data series to a **Stacked Area** data series

8. **Delete** the **Area** data series

9. Create a **Legend** to the right of the chart

10. Change the **Major** units used on the **Vertical Axis** to 3500.0

11. Save the workbook as **Chart**

Summary

Charts

In this section, you have learned how to:

- Format secondary axes, data series, and scale of value axis in charts

- Apply, edit, and format data labels in charts

- Change chart types to column, bar, area, line, pie, and combo charts

Section 4

Analysis

In this section, you will learn:

- PivotTables and how to summarise information

- Sorting and filtering columns in tables

- Scenarios and how to predict future financial outcomes

Pivot Tables

Pivot Tables arrange and summarise data from a table that has labelled columns. Usually, two fields from the data mark the column and row headings. The table represents information in different ways.

For instance, if you have a table of staff details with headings, a pivot table compares pay rates for staff working in different departments. Pivot Tables summarise information, e.g., finding the number of people working in a particular department with specific salaries. The values can be added together, counted, and averaged.

1. Open the workbook **Staff List**

2. Click inside the table

3. On the **Insert** tab, locate the **Tables** group, select **Pivot Table**

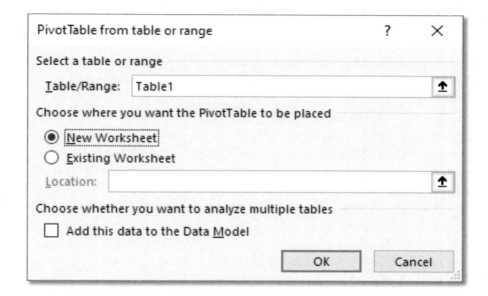

4. For **Choose where to place the Pivot Table,** click on **New Worksheet**

5. In the **Create Pivot Table** dialog box, click on **OK**

6. Name the worksheet as **PivotTable**

7. On the **Pivot Table Fields** pane, click and drag **First Name** to **Rows, Department** to **Columns** and **Gender** to **Values**

8. The **Pivot Table** will give a summary of employee genders by department

9. Switch **First Name** to **Columns** and **Department** to **Rows**

10. The **Pivot Table** shows employee names along the top and departments along the right

11. Click & drag **First Name** to **Values** and move **Gender** to **Columns**

Count of Gender	Column Labels		
Row Labels	F	M	Grand Total
Administration	1	3	4
Marketing	2	1	3
Reception	1	1	2
Sales		5	5
Grand Total	4	10	14

12. The **PivotTable** now displays a summary of **Employees** in each **Department** based on **Gender**

13. Save the workbook and leave it open

Modify the Data Source

The information for the Pivot Table updates to reflect any changes made to the original data. For instance, if there are updates to salaries for employees, the data can be changed in the original table and updated in the Pivot Table

1. Open the workbook **Staff List**

2. Return to the **Staff List** worksheet and enter the following details:

    James, Smith, M, 15/04/1975, Waterfront, Administration

3. Return to the **PivotTable** worksheet

4. On the **Pivot Table Analyse** tab, select **Refresh**

5. The **Pivot Table** updates

6. Return to the **Staff** worksheet and delete the added entry from the table

7. On the **Pivot Table Analyse** tab in the **Data** group, select **Refresh**

8. The **Pivot Table** updates to include the additional entry

9. Save the workbook and leave it open

Filter & Sort a Pivot Table

A filter in a Pivot Table can show separate categories. The table displays only required information, e.g. the average salary for employees in the marketing department. You can sort details such as surnames in ascending or descending alphabetical order.

1. Open the workbook **Staff List**

2. Click on the arrow beside the **Row Labels** heading

3. Click on the **Select All** checkbox to deselect the different departments

4. Select the **Sales** checkbox and click **OK**

5. It filters the table displaying employees in the **Sales** department

6. Click on the **Row Labels** arrow again and click on **Select All** and click **OK**

7. This setting shows all the employees working in each department

8. Click on the arrow beside the **Row Labels** heading

9. Sort the **Row Labels** by clicking on **Sort A to Z**

10. The list is sorted in alphabetical order by **Department**

11. Click on the **Row Labels** arrow and hover over **Label Filters**

12. Select **Equals**

13. Enter **F** for the **Label Filter** value

14. Click **OK**

15. It sorts the table by **Department** in **Ascending Order** for **Female** employees

16. Save the workbook and leave it open

Grouping Data

Grouping data in a Pivot Table displays related information together. This feature compares information in a data source. For instance, you may want to combine two departments in your organisation and compare them with another group of departments. This information can then help assess the performance of departments in a company.

1. Open the workbook **Staff List** and display the **PivotTable** worksheet

2. On the **PivotTable Analyze** tab in the **Actions** group, select the **Clear** arrow and choose **Clear Filters**

3. Select the **Administration** and **Reception** departments while holding down the **Ctrl** key

4. On the **PivotTable Analyse** tab in the **Group**, click on **Group Selection**

5. Select cell A5 **Group1** and use the **Formula Bar** to rename the group **Admin**

6. Group the **Sales** and **Marketing** departments and name them **Sales**

7. Save the workbook as **Pivot Table** and close it

One Input Data Table

A data table shows how altering one variable in a formula affects the result of that formula, e.g. calculating the amount of interest on a savings account at different interest rates. The monthly repayment amount stays the same while calculating different interest rates. Rather than typing in several formulas for each interest rate, a data table calculates this information automatically. It is an efficient way of calculating variable amounts using formulas.

1. Open the **Repayments on Loan** workbook

2. Highlight cells B9:B19

3. On the **Home** tab in the **Editing** group, select **Series**

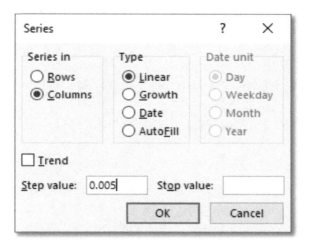

4. Under **Series In** select **Columns**

5. For **Type** select **Linear**

6. For **Step Value,** enter **0.005**

7. Click **OK**

8. This input will create a variable interest rate that increases by 0.5% for each calculation

9. This feature calculates the loan amount based on different interest rates

10. In cell C8, type in **=B6**

11. Highlight cells B8:C19

12. On the **Data** tab in the **Forecast** group, select **What-If Analysis** and choose **Data Table**

13. Highlight cell B4 for the **Column Input Cell**

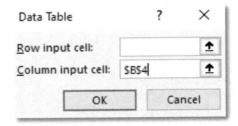

14. This input uses the standard interest rate on the loan to calculate the variable interest rate in the data table

15. Click **OK**

16. Change the cell range C9:C19 to currency with two decimal places

17. The **Data Table** will calculate the monthly repayments based on variable interest rates

18. Save the workbook as **Loan**

Two Input Data Table

A two-input data table shows how changing two variables in a formula affects the result of that formula, e.g. calculating the amount of interest on a savings account at variable interest rates at different periods. The interest rate variable changes and the length of the savings period also changes. It produces a different amount depending on changing interest rates and different periods. A two-input data table uses two changing variables compared with one changing variable in a one-input data table.

1. Open the workbook **Loan**

2. Delete the contents of cells in the range C9:C19

3. Cut and paste the **PMT** value to cell B8

4. Enter 12 into cell C8

5. Highlight cells C8:G8

6. On the **Home** tab in the **Editing** group, select **Series**

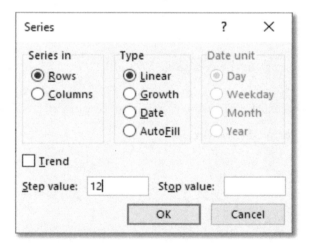

7. Under **Series In** select **Rows**

8. Under **Type** select **Linear**

9. For **Step Value**, enter 12

10. Click **OK**

11. The fill series creates the loan period in increments of 12 months

12. Highlight cells B8:G19

13. On the **Data** tab in the **Forecast** group, click on **What-If Analysis** and choose **Data Table**

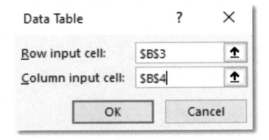

14. Select cell B3 for the **Row Input Cell**

15. It includes the loan period in the data table calculation

16. Select cell B4 for the **Column Input Cell**

17. It includes the interest rate in the data table calculation

18. Click **OK**

19. Apply a currency format to the cell range C9:G19

20. A **Data Table** displays the monthly repayment amount depending on a variable interest rate and a variable term of the loan

21. Save the workbook and close it

Sorting

Sorting applies to tables of information in many ways. Data can be sorted alphabetically, starting with one column and then sorted in descending order in another. For example, you may have a table containing the first names and surnames of employees. The table is sorted by the first selected column and then by the second column. The table sorts by surname in ascending order and then by the first name in descending order.

1. Open the **Customer Details** workbook

2. Highlight the cells A2:C11

3. On the **Home** tab in the **Editing** group, select **Sort & Filter**

4. Select **Custom Sort**

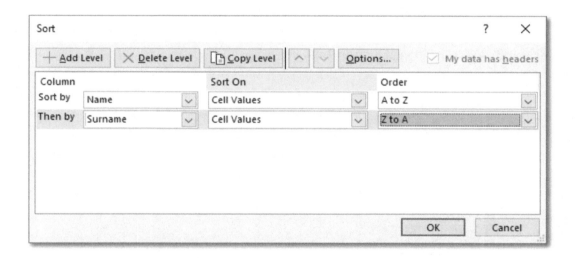

5. Sort by **Name** in **Ascending Order**

6. Click on the **Add Level** button and then sort by **Surname** in **Descending Order**

7. Click **OK**

8. The table has sorted by **Name** in **Ascending Alphabetical Order** and then by **Surname** in **Descending Alphabetical Order**

9. Save the workbook as **Sort** and leave it open

Custom List

A custom list allows you to develop a unique list for a column of data. For instance, if a list of car manufacturers is to be included in a list, creating a custom list can make putting information into a table more efficient.

1. Open the **Sort** workbook

2. Highlight cell A2:D11

3. On the **Home** tab in the **Editing** group, click on **Sort & Filter**

4. Select **Custom Sort**

5. Click on the **Delete Level** button to delete the other custom sorts

6. Click on the **Add Level** button and choose **Day of Birth**

7. Select **Order** and choose **Custom List**

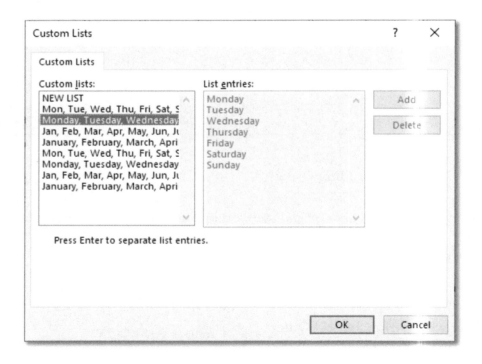

8. Select the **Custom List** Monday, Tuesday, Wednesday...

9. Click **OK**

10. Click **OK** again

11. The **Day of Birth** list sorts by **Ascending Order**

12. Save the workbook and close it

Filter

A filter applies to data in a table, so only selected information appears. For instance, if you want to show employees working in the marketing department in a list of staff, a filter can show only marketing employees.

1. Open the workbook **Filter**

2. Highlight cells A1:C11

3. On the **Home** tab in the **Editing** group, click on **Sort & Filter**

4. Select **Filter**

5. Click on the arrow beside **Department**

6. Select the check box **Select All**

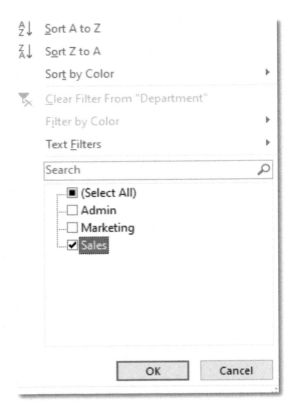

7. Select the **Sales** check box

8. Click **OK**

9. It filters the table to display employees in the **Sales** department

10. Highlight the table

11. On the **Home** tab, select **Sort & Filter**

12. Select **Clear**

13. Select the **Age** column filter

14. Hover over **Number Filters** and choose **Custom Filters**

15. For **Age,** choose **Is Greater Than** and enter 34

16. Select **And**

17. Choose **Is Less Than** and enter 60

18. Click **OK**

19. It will filter the table to display staff between the ages of 34 and 60

20. **Clear** the filter

21. Save the workbook and leave it open

Advanced Filter

You can filter information in a table based on specific criteria. For instance, if you want to filter a table to show details from the sales department and only for employees older than thirty, you apply an advanced filter.

1. With the **Filter** workbook open, insert two rows above the table

2. Copy A3:C3 to A1:C1

3. In cell B2, enter **>30**

4. In cell C2, enter **Sales**

5. On the **Data** tab in the **Sort & Filter** group, click on **Advanced**

6. Under **Action,** select **Copy to another location**

7. For **List Range,** select the table A3:C13

8. For **Criteria Range** select A1:C2

9. For **Copy to** select A15

10. A filter based on Sales department employees over the age of **30** appears

11. Click **OK** and save the workbook

Outline

An outline hides parts of a worksheet enabling you to view the specific parts of a table. This feature compares groups of information in a table. An outline can show up to eight different levels horizontally and vertically. Outlines allow you to view a table's main parts, such as the total income or gross profit.

1. Open the workbook **Group**

2. Select any cell in the table

3. On the **Data** tab, select **Outline,** click on **Group** and choose **Auto Outline**

4. Click on the **Top Minus Button** to the left of the table to hide the **Income Sources** in the table

5. Click on the **Middle Minus Button** to display only the **Total Expenses** for each month

1 2 3		A	B	C	D	E	F	G
	1		Jan	Feb	Mar	Apr	May	Jun
	4	Total Income	€ 1,550	€ 1,575	€ 1,650	€ 1,575	€ 1,525	€ 1,575
	5							
	6	Mortgage	€ 600	€ 600	€ 600	€ 600	€ 600	€ 600
	7	Electricity		€ 145			€ 125	
	8	Telephone	€ 30	€ 30	€ 30	€ 30	€ 30	€ 30
	9	Food	€ 350	€ 400	€ 325	€ 300	€ 450	€ 350
	10	Leisure	€ 150	€ 250	€ 300	€ 125	€ 75	€ 350
	11	Total Expenses	€ 1,130	€ 1,425	€ 1,255	€ 1,055	€ 1,280	€ 1,330
	12	Savings	€ 420	€ 150	€ 395	€ 520	€ 245	€ 750
	13							

(Formula bar: A2 — fx Salary)

6. Click on the **Level 3 number** located at the top left of the table to display the entire table

7. Click on the **Level 1 number** to display only the total **Savings** for each month

8. Select **Level 2** to display total **Income, Expenses** and **Savings**

Manual Outline

1. Display the entire table

2. Select rows 6 to 8

3. On the **Data** tab, click on **Outline,** then **Group**

4. It manually groups the **Mortgage, Electricity** & **Telephone** rows together

5. Select rows 9 and 10

6. On the **Data** tab, click on **Outline,** then **Group**

7. It groups the **Expenses** together

8. Select rows 6 to 8

9. On the **Data** tab, click on **Outline,** then **Ungroup**

10. It has ungrouped the selected data

11. On the **Data** tab, click on **Outline** and select **Ungroup**

12. Click on **Clear Outline**

13. The worksheet is ungrouped

14. Save the workbook and leave it open

Subtotals

Subtotals calculate the total of groups of values and summarise this information. Options for calculating subtotals include displaying averages in groups and multiplying numerical values. For instance, if you have a sales worksheet and want to find the subtotals of monthly sales, the subtotals feature shows totals for each month.

1. Open the **Group** workbook

2. Highlight cells B1:B12

3. On the **Data** tab, select **Outline** and click on **Subtotal**

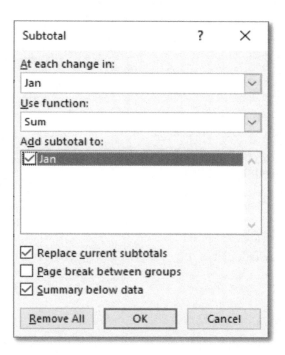

4. Under **Add Subtotal To** select **Jan**

5. Click **OK**

6. Subtotals calculate the January total

7. Highlight cell C4

8. On the **Data** tab, click on **Outline** and select **Subtotal**

9. For **At Each Change In** select **Jan**

10. Under **Use Function,** select **Average**

11. Under **Add Subtotal To** select **Jan**

12. Click **OK**

13. The subtotal feature calculates the average **Salary, Other Income** and **Total Income** for **January**

14. Save the workbook and close it

Scenarios

Scenarios predict future outcomes based on current data in a worksheet. Scenarios forecast results based on different amounts. For instance, you can indicate how company profits will rise or fall depending on variable sales.

1. Open the workbook **Scenarios**

2. Highlight B3:B5

3. On the **Data** tab in the **Forecast** group, click on **What-If Analysis** and choose **Scenario Manager**

4. For **Scenario Name,** enter **Worst Case** and click **OK**

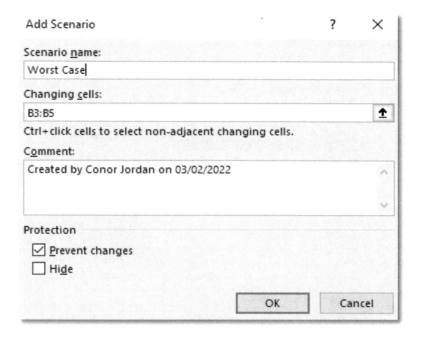

5. Under **Please enter a value** enter 0 for each cell

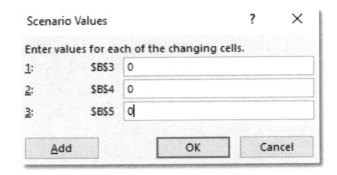

6. Click **Add**

7. For **Scenario Name,** enter **Expected** and click **OK**

8. Type in 1500,1800 & 2500 and click on **Add**

9. Enter a **Scenario Name** of **Best Case** and click **OK**

10. Type in 3500, 3800 & 4000 and click **OK**

11. Select the **Expected** scenario

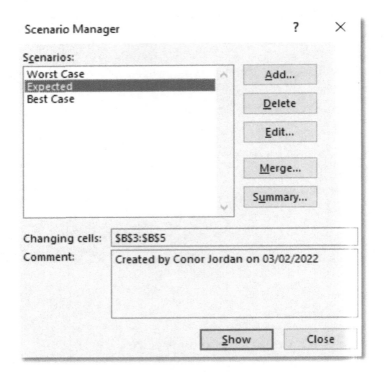

12. Click on **Merge**

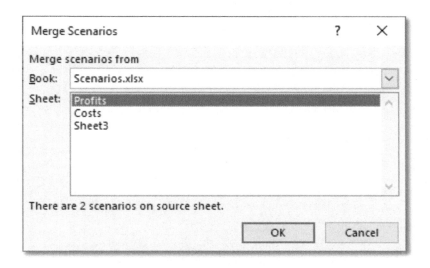

13. Under **Merge Scenarios From** select **Scenarios.xlsx**

14. Select the **Profits** worksheet and click **OK**

15. The **Best Case** and **Worst Case** scenarios from the **Profits** worksheet appear

16. Open the **Scenario Manager** dialog box again

17. Highlight the **Best Case** scenario from the **Profits** worksheet

18. Click on the **Delete** button

19. You have deleted the **Best Case** scenario

20. Select **Worst Case** at the bottom and click **Edit**

21. Rename the scenario as **Expected 2**

22. Click **OK**

23. Type in 200, 300 & 400

24. Click **OK**

25. Highlight the **Best Case** scenario and select **Show**

26. The selected values in a **Best Case** scenario appear

27. Show the **Expected** and **Worst Case** scenarios using the **Show** feature

28. Click on **Summary**

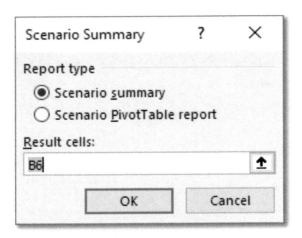

28. Choose **Report Type** as **Scenario Summary**

29. Enter the **Result Cells** as B6

30. Click **OK**

31. It creates a **Scenario Summary** report

32. Save the workbook and close it

Revision - Section 4

1. Open the **Employees** workbook

2. Create a **Pivot Table** named **Staff** with the **Department** field for columns, **Surname** for Rows and Count of **Gender** as Values

3. Switch **Surname** to **Columns** and **Department** to **Rows**

4. Enter the following details in **Row 13** of the **Employees** table:

   George, Hughes, M, 12/7/1984, Ross, Marketing

5. **Update** the PivotTable

6. **Filter** the **Rows** by **Department** displaying Marketing

7. **Clear** the filter

8. Group the **Administration** and **Reception** departments and name them **Admin**

9. Group the **Marketing** & **Sales** departments and name it **Sales**

10. **Sort** the table by **Surname Ascending**

11. **Filter** the table to show only the **Admin** department

12. Save the workbook as **Pivot**

13. Open the **Monthly Repayments** workbook

14. Display the **Data Table** worksheet

15. Create a **Data Table** showing the monthly repayments over each successive year at each percentage with a currency format

16. Save and close the workbook

17. Open the **Group** workbook

18. Apply an **Auto Outline** to the table

19. Highlight cells B1:B12 and create **Subtotals** using the Sum function for January

20. Clear the table outline

21. Create a **Best Case Scenario** where total income in January, February & March that will be €1,000, €1,200, and €1,500, and a **Worst Case Scenario** where income will be €500, €450, and €350, respectively

22. Create a **Scenario Summary** of this information

23. Save the workbook and close it

Summary

Analysis

In this section, you have learned how to:

- Create and modify PivotTables to summarise information

- Sort and filter columns based on their values

- Predict future financial outcomes using scenarios

Section 5

Validating & Auditing

In this section, you will learn:

- Data Validation to limit information entry into tables

- Auditing features such as tracing precedents, dependants & errors

- Creating, editing, deleting, and showing comments

Data Validation

Data validation can reduce the risk of errors occurring in a worksheet. Data validation restricts information entry into cells prompting the worksheet user to enter the correct information. It applies restrictions to forms or templates that can accept input in some cells.

1. Open the workbook **Data Validation**

2. Highlight cells B4:B10

3. On the **Data** tab in the **Data Tools** group, select **Data Validation**

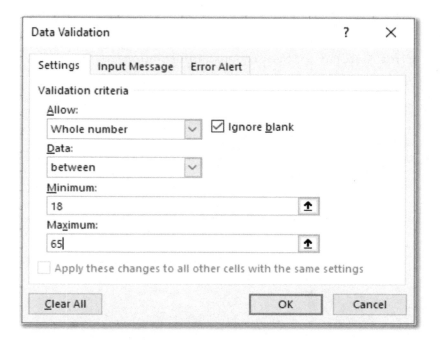

4. Allow **Whole Numbers**

5. For **Data** choose **Between**

6. For **Minimum** enter 18 and **Maximum** 65

7. On the **Input Message** tab, type in **Enter Age** for **Title**

8. In **Input Message** enter **Please enter an age between 18-65**

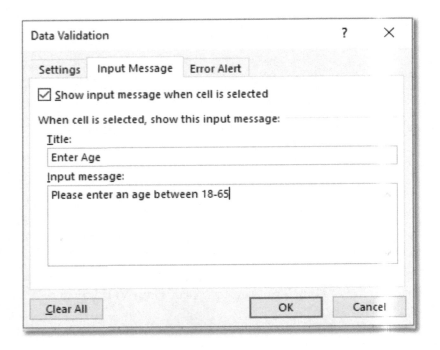

9. On the **Error Alert** tab, for **Style,** choose **Information**

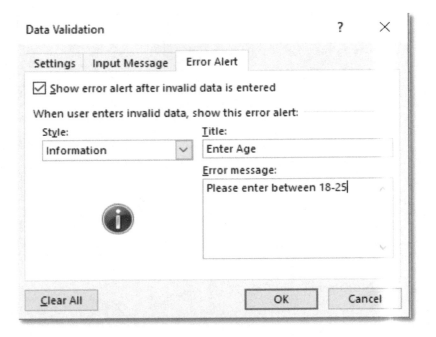

10. On the **Error Alert** tab, for **Style,** choose **Information**

11. For **Title** type in **Enter Age**

12. For **Error Message** type, **Please enter between 18-25**

13. Click **OK**

14. Try and type 70 for cell B7

15. The **Error Message** will appear

16. Click **OK**

17. On the **Data** tab in the **Data Tools** group, select the arrow beside **Data Validation**

18. Choose **Circle Invalid Data**

19. It will circle all data that does not follow the **Data Validation** settings

20. On the **Data** tab, select the arrow beside **Data Validation**

21. Choose **Clear Validation Circles**

22. It removes data circles in the worksheet

23. On the **Data** tab, choose **Data Validation**

24. In the **Data Validation** dialog box, click on the **Clear All** button

25. Click **OK**

26. It removes data validation from the worksheet

27. Highlight cells D4:D10

28. On the **Data** tab, select **Data Validation**

29. Under **Validation Criteria** for **Allow** choose **List**

30. Click in the **Source** textbox and select cells **A12:A14**

31. Type in an **Input Message Title** of **Enter Department**

32. Include an **Input Message** of **Choose the correct department**

33. Include a **Warning** style prompt with the same **Title** and **Message** as the **Input Message**

34. Click **OK**

35. Click on cell D4

36. There is now a drop-down list containing department names for the cells D4:D10

37. Choose the **Admin** department for cell D4

38. Highlight cells H4:H10

39. Select **Data Validation** and for **Allow** choose **Decimal**

40. Allow values **Between** a **Minimum** of 18500 and a **Maximum** of 23000

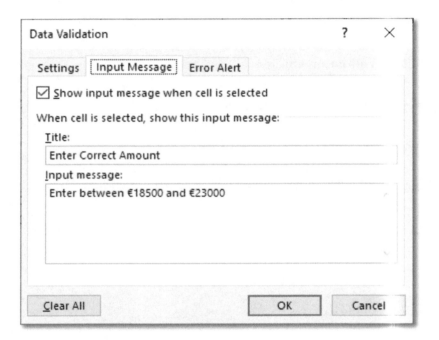

41. Enter an **Input Message** of **Enter Correct Amount** for the **Title** and **Enter between €18500 and €23000** for the **Input Message**

42. Enter the same **Title** and **Input Message** for the **Error Alert** and choose a **Style** of **Stop**

43. Click **OK**

44. Try and enter a value of €18000 into cell H5. A dialog prompt appears. Click on **Retry**

45. Now enter a value of €19500. It is allowed

46. Highlight cells I4:I10

47. Select **Data Validation** and for **Allow** choose **Date**

48. Allow a date that is **Less than or Equal to** 31/12/1980

49. Only dates of birth that are before this date are allowed

50. Enter in an appropriate **Input Message** and **Error Alert**

51. Click **OK**

52. Try entering a birth date in cell I4 after 31/12/1980

53. Excel will prompt you to change the date

54. Enter in the date 3/1/1979

55. The date entry is allowed

56. Select the cell range J4:J10

57. Display the **Data Validation** dialog box

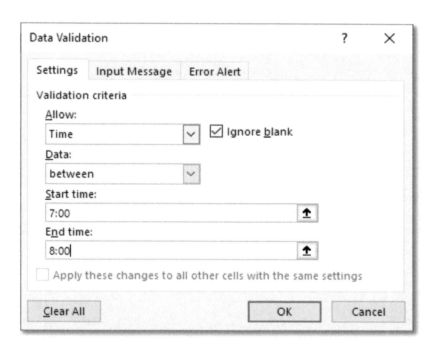

58. For **Allow** choose **Time**

59. On the **Settings** tab, enter in a **Start Time** of 7:00

60. Enter in an **End Time** of 8:00

61. Enter in an appropriate **Input Message** and **Error Alert**

62. Click **OK**

63. In cell J4 enter in 9:00

64. It will not be allowed, and Excel prompts you to enter the correct time

65. Enter 7:30

66. It is allowed

67. Save the workbook and leave it open

Tracing Precedents & Dependents

You can trace cells containing formulas to check for errors. The tracing precedents feature allows you to determine the values included in a selected formula. The tracing dependents feature lets you view what cells are affected by a formula. It helps you check why a formula might have an error allowing you to make changes.

1. Open the workbook **Tracing Precedents & Dependents**

2. Select cell C5

3. On the **Formulas** tab in the **Formula Auditing** group, select **Trace Precedents**

4. An arrow shows where the formula in cell C5 originated, in this case, cell C3 minus cell C4

5. Select cell D3

6. On the **Formulas** tab in the **Formula Auditing** group, select **Trace Dependents**

7. An arrow appears showing the formula's path, in this case, cell D3 minus cell D4

8. Select cell I5 and type in =

9. Move to the **Profit Loss 2** worksheet

10. Select cell I5

11. Press **Enter**

12. On the **Formulas** tab, choose **Trace Precedents**

13. An arrow with a worksheet icon will appear, showing a link to the formula involving the other worksheet

14. Double-click on the **Arrow,** and it will display the following dialog box

15. Select the first **Go To** entry

16. The worksheet shows where the formula has originated

17. Click **OK**

18. The formulas in cell I5 on the **Profit Loss 2** worksheet appear

19. Save the workbook and leave it open

Tracing Errors

Tracing errors helps when collaborating with another person using the same spreadsheet. Excel traces errors to where they originated, allowing you to determine where a fault in the formula may be. You then can change the formula to correct the mistake.

1. Open the workbook **Tracing Precedents & Dependents**

2. Select cell C8

3. On the **Formulas** tab in the **Formula Auditing** group, select the arrow beside **Error Checking** and choose **Trace Error**

4. Tracing errors allows you to see what cells are causing the error in the formula

5. In this case, the error is the zero value in cell C7

6. On the **Formulas** tab, select **Show Formulas**

7. All formulas in the worksheet appear

8. Click on the **Show Formulas** button again

9. Enter 3000 into cell C7

10. A target performance of 67% shows in cell C8

11. On the **Formulas** tab in the **Formula Auditing** group, select **Remove Arrows**

12. Save the workbook and close it

Comments

Comments enable communication between collaborators and help identify parts of a spreadsheet that may need attention. When collaborating with others on a spreadsheet, comments can be added to specific cells and edited. For example, if there are low sales in June, a comment can be added by one user, viewed, edited by another user and deleted when no longer needed.

1. Open the **Tracing & Dependants** workbook

2. Select cell D3

3. On the **Review** tab in the **Comments** group located to the left of the **Ribbon**, select **New Comment**

4. Enter in the comment "Sales need to be higher."

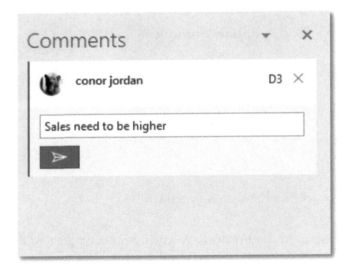

5. Click on the **Post** icon to create the comment

6. On the **Review** tab, select **Show Comments**

7. On the **Review** tab, choose **Show Comments** again

8. Display all comments again

9. Select cell G5

10. On the **Review** tab in the **Comments** group, select **New Comment**

11. Type "Performance was down this month."

12. Click on the **Post** icon to create the comment

13. Select cell G5 again

14. Click on **Edit**

15. Edit the text to read, "Performance was lower than usual this month."

16. In the **Comments** group, select **Previous Comment**

17. On the **Comments** pane, click inside the **Reply** textbox and type "I agree, more sales." in cell D3

18. With cell D3 selected, on the **Comments** group, click on **Delete**

19. Deletion removes the comment in cell D3

20. Select cell G5

21. On the **Comments** pane, select the three dots on the top right of the comment

22. Select **Resolve Thread**

23. Resolving the comments ends further communication about this cell

24. Click on **Delete Thread**

25. It has removed the comment in cell G5 from the worksheet

26. Save the workbook and close it

Revision - Section 5

1. Open the **Employee Record** workbook

2. Highlight cells F3:F15

3. Apply **Data Validation** that only allows whole numbers above 65 to be entered

4. Enter an appropriate **Input Message** and **Error Alert**

5. Attempt to enter a value of 50 into cell F3

6. Circle the invalid data

7. Correct the error by entering 104 into cell F3

8. Save the workbook as **Validated**

9. Open the **Calculated** workbook

10. Trace the **Precedents** of cell B7

11. Trade the **Dependents** of cell B4

12. Display **All Formulas** on the worksheet

13. Hide **All Formulas** on the worksheet

14. Add a **Comment** to cell B7 with the text "This amount should be higher."

15. Reply to the **Comment** in cell B7 with the text "I agree, this amount should be higher."

16. **Resolve** the thread, then **Delete** the thread

17. Save the workbook as **Audited**

Summary

Validating & Auditing

In this section, you have learned how to:

- Apply data validation to limit data entry in tables

- Auditing of formulas by tracing precedents, dependents, and errors

- Create, edit, resolve, reply to, and delete comments in a worksheet

Section 6

Excel Productivity

In this section, you will learn:

- Applying names to groups of data and formulas

- Paste special and its applications

- Creating and running macros

Defining Names

Groups of related data in a spreadsheet can be labelled. Named groups are included in formulas to make calculations easier to identify. Instead of having cell references, named groups become part of formulas. For example, =Total Income - Total Expenses is used rather than =B6 - B12

1. Open the workbook **Naming Cells**

2. Select the range A4:G4

3. On the **Formulas** tab in the **Defined Names** group, select **Define Name**

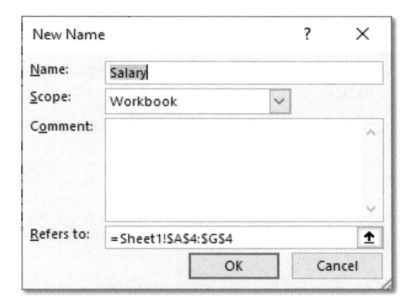

4. In the **Name** textbox, enter **Salary**

5. Click **OK**

6. Select rows 8, 9 & 10

7. On the **Formulas** tab, select **Create from Selection**

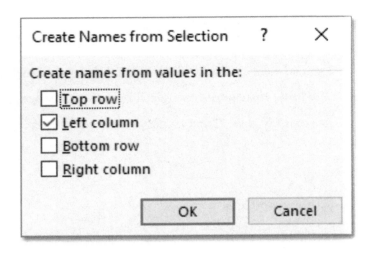

8. Select the **Left Column** checkbox and click **OK**

9. Left column headings are named

10. Select rows 6, 11 & 12

11. On the **Formulas** tab, select **Create from Selection**

12. Select the **Left Column** checkbox and click **OK**

13. Names apply to selected headings

14. On the **Formulas** tab in the **Defined Names** group, select **Name Manager**

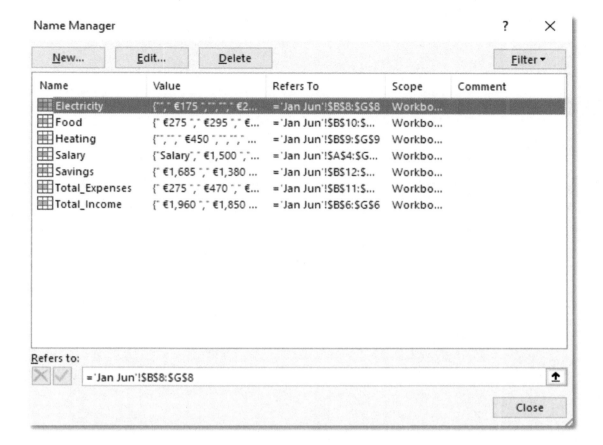

15. Select **New**

16. Enter a name of **Income** and click **OK**

17. Highlight the **Savings** name and select **Edit**

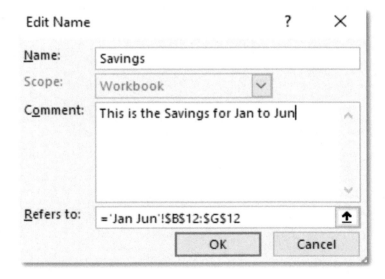

18. Enter in a comment of "This is the Savings for Jan to Jun."

19. Click **OK**

20. Highlight the **Income** defined name and click on the **Delete** button

21. Click **OK**

22. Save the workbook as **Naming Cells**

Using Names in a Function

Names are used in functions to make them clearer. For example, rather than having a formula such as A1-A2=A3, with names in a function, the formula could be expressed as Income-Expenses=Net Profit

1. With the workbook still open, select cell B12

2. Type in the **Equals** sign

3. Begin typing "To", and the named range **Total_Income** will appear

4. Double-click on **Total_Income**

5. Type in a **Minus** sign

6. Begin typing "To", and the named range **Total_Expenditure** will appear

7. Double-click on **Total_Expenditure**

8. Press **Enter**

9. The formula calculates the savings amount

10. Save the workbook and leave it open

Activate, deactivate the group mode

Group mode applies when you want worksheets joined. When copying and moving information between worksheets and other workbooks, grouped worksheets are treated as a single worksheet. There is an option to activate and deactivate group mode.

1. With the workbook open, select the **Jan Jun** worksheet

2. Hold down **Alt+Ctrl** and select the **Jul Dec** worksheet

3. The workbook is now in **Group Mode**

4. Group mode allows changes made in the active worksheets to apply to other worksheets

5. Right-click on the grouped worksheets and select **Move or Copy**

6. For **To Book** select **(new book)**

7. Select **Create a Copy** and click **OK**

8. The grouped worksheets copies to a new workbook

9. Delete the new workbook

10. Right-click on the grouped worksheets

11. Select **Ungroup Sheets**

12. **Group Mode** is now deactivated

13. Save the workbook and close it

Paste Special

Paste special is used to copy data with different options, e.g. paste only values without copying original formulas. This feature allows you to copy and paste information without making an exact copy of the selected data. Paste special can also combine a range of cells by adding, subtracting, dividing, or multiplying their values. You can combine two ranges of cells on different worksheets with paste special.

1. With the **Naming Cells** workbook still open, copy B4:G6 in the **Jan Jun** worksheet

2. Move to the following worksheet and select cells B4:G6

3. On the **Home** tab, click on the drop-down arrow under the **Paste** button and choose **Paste Special**

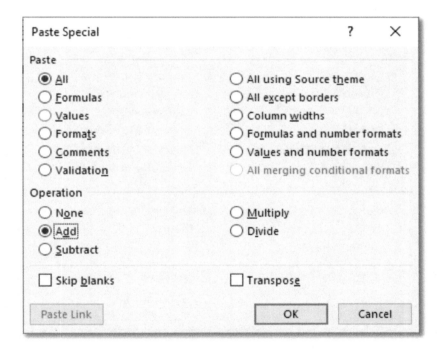

4. Under **Operation,** choose **Add**

5. Click **OK**

6. The paste special operation **Adds** the selected cells in both worksheets

7. Copy B4:G6 in the **Jan Jun** worksheet

8. Move to the following worksheet and select cells B4:G6

9. On the **Home** tab, click on the drop-down arrow beside **Paste** and choose **Paste Special**

10. Under **Operation,** choose **Subtract**

11. The **Subtract** operation subtracts the first worksheet from the second and returns them to their original values

12. With the **Naming Cells** workbook still open, copy B14 in the **Jan Jun** worksheet

13. Move to the next worksheet and select cell B14

14. On the **Home** tab, click on the drop-down arrow under the **Paste** button and choose **Paste Special**

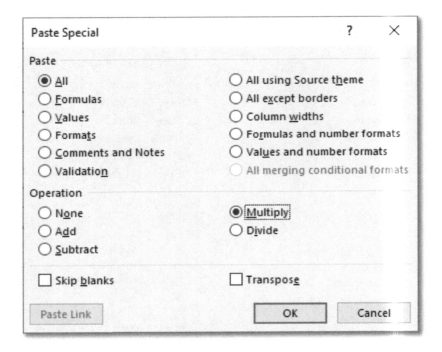

15. Under **Operation,** choose **Multiply**

16. Click **OK**

17. The calculation multiplies **15%** by the **Total Savings**

18. With the **Naming Cells** workbook still open, copy cell B14 in the **Jan Jun** worksheet

19. Move to the following worksheet and select cell B14

20. On the **Home** tab, click on the drop-down arrow under the **Paste** button and choose **Paste Special**

21. Under **Operation** choose **Divide**

22. The division calculation divides the **Shareholder Dividends** by 15%

23. Save the workbook and leave it open

Pasting Values

Paste special can copy and paste only the values without any original formulas. The pasting values option makes no changes to the copied values within a range of cells.

1. With the **Jan Jun** worksheet open, copy the cell range A3:G12

2. On **Sheet3**, select cell A3 and open the **Paste Special** dialog box

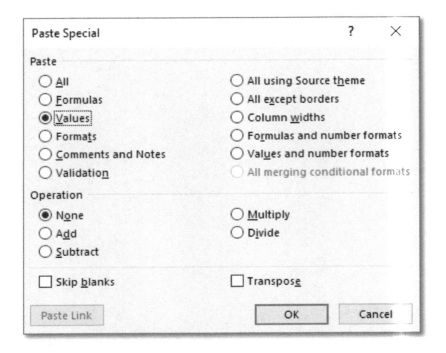

3. Under **Paste** select **Values** and click on **OK**

4. Only cell values appear in the worksheet

5. Select cell B6

6. Notice that there are no formulas in the **Formulas** bar

7. In the **Sheet1** worksheet, copy the cells B6:G6

8. Select cell I3

9. Click on the **Paste** drop-down arrow and select **Paste Special**

10. Select the **Transpose** checkbox

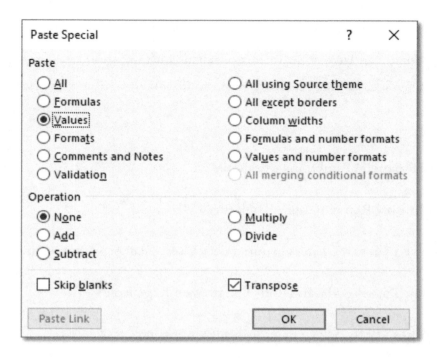

11. Click **OK**

12. You have copied the **Total Income** row into the selected column

13. Save the workbook and close it

Hyperlinks

Hyperlinks link the contents of a cell to another cell, worksheet, workbook, or website. Linking applies when working with large spreadsheets or when you want to link to an external website. Simply click the hyperlink, and the cell, worksheet, workbook, or website displays.

1. Open the **Financial Functions** workbook

2. On the **Monthly Repayments** tab, select cell D1

3. On the **Insert** tab in the **Links group,** select **Link** and choose **Insert Link**

4. Under **Link To:** select the **Existing File or Web Page** icon

5. In the **Address** textbox, type in www.digidiscover.com

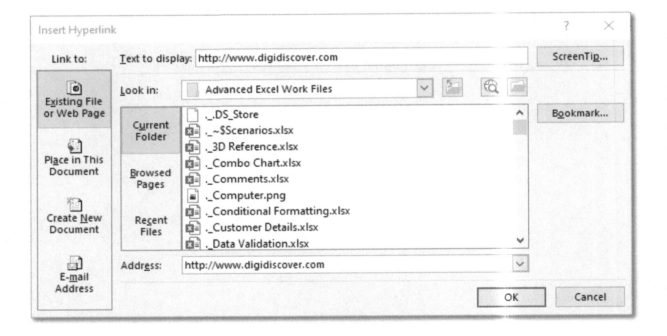

6. Click **OK**

7. Click on the link in cell D1, and if connected to the internet, this author's website should appear in your browser

8. Right-click on cell D1

9. Choose **Edit Hyperlink**

10. Select **Place In This Document**

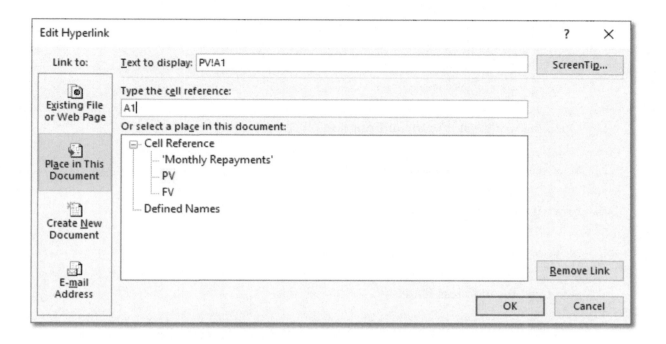

11. For **Type the cell reference,** enter A1

12. Select **PV** for **Or select a place in this document**

13. Click **OK**

14. A link between both worksheets form

15. Right-click on the hyperlink in D1 on the **Monthly Repayments** tab

16. Choose **Remove Hyperlink**

17. There is no longer a link in the **PV** worksheet

18. Close the workbook without saving

Link Data Between Spreadsheets

Data links between worksheets and spreadsheets when specific settings are applied. Information in one worksheet links to data in another worksheet. When both worksheets contain related information, such as a budget, you can use linking.

1. Open the workbook **Financial Functions**

2. Select cell B5 on the **Monthly Repayments** tab

3. Enter **Equals**

4. Move to the **PV** worksheet

5. Select cell B5 and press **Enter**

6. A link has been created between cell B5 on the **Monthly Repayments** tab and B5 on the **PV** worksheet

7. Open the **Mathematical Functions** workbook

8. Select cell G4 and type in **Equals**

9. Make the **Financial Functions** workbook active

10. Select cell B5 and press **Enter**

11. Establishing a link between the loan amount in the **Financial Functions** workbook and the **PMT** amount in the **Mathematical Functions** workbook connects both cells

12. Change the value in B4 on the **Financial Functions** workbook to €25,000

13. Display the **Mathematical Functions** workbook

14. The savings amount for January in cell C4 updates

15. Save the spreadsheet and leave it open

Break Links

Links can be broken between worksheets if you do not want further connections to remain. Removing links apply when there is no longer a need to have a link between both worksheets.

1. With both workbooks open, on the **Data** tab in the **Queries & Connections** group, select **Edit Links**

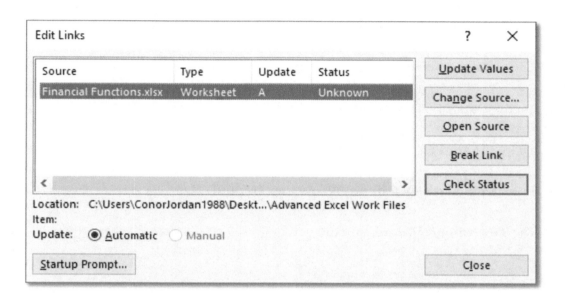

2. Select **Break Link**

3. Choose **Break Links**

4. Click **Close**

5. The link between both workbooks no longer exists

6. Save both workbooks and close them

Importing Delimited Data

Data imported into a spreadsheet appears in various formats, such as a text file without proper separators (Spaces, Tabs, Commas). For example, a text file containing contact details separated by commas can be imported into a spreadsheet busing delimited data.

1. Open the **Employees Details.txt** file from your work files folder

2. Notice how records are separated using commas

3. Create a new workbook

4. On the **Data** tab in the **Get & Transform Data** group, click on **Get Data**

5. Choose **From File**, select **From Text/CSV**

6. Select **Employees Details.txt** file and click **Import**

7. The **Text Import Wizard** appears

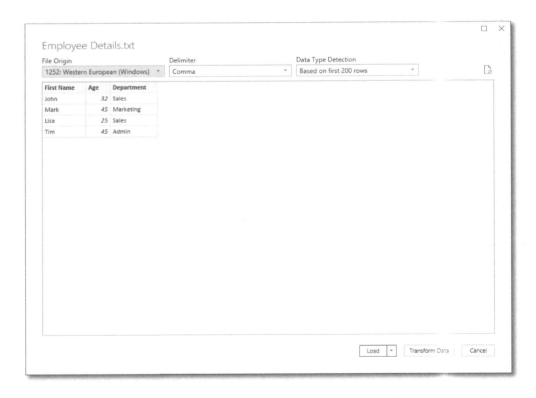

8. Under **Delimiter,** choose **Comma**

9. Click on **Load**

10. The table appears in the spreadsheet

11. Save the workbook as **Imported Data** and close it

Record a Macro

A Macro is a series of commands that can be recorded and played back to carry out tasks automatically. Macros are useful for repetitive tasks performed repeatedly. You simply run the macro, and the recorded tasks repeat.

1. Open the workbook **Macro**

2. To the right of the **Quick Access Toolbar,** select **Customize Quick Access Toolbar**

3. Select **More Commands**

4. Select the **Customize Ribbon** tab

5. Choose **Main Tabs**

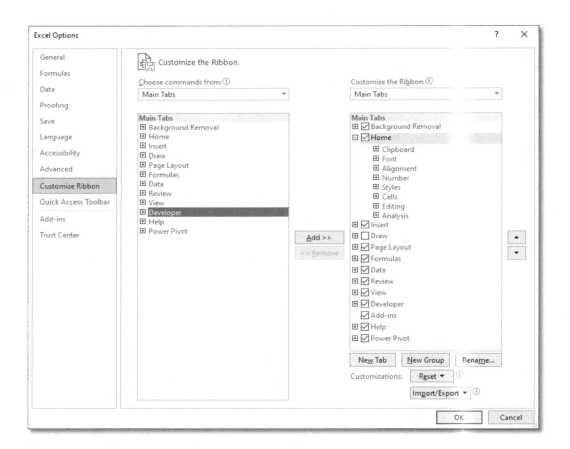

6. Select **Developer** and click the **Add** button

7. Click **OK**

8. On the **Developer** tab in the **Code** group, select **Record Macro**

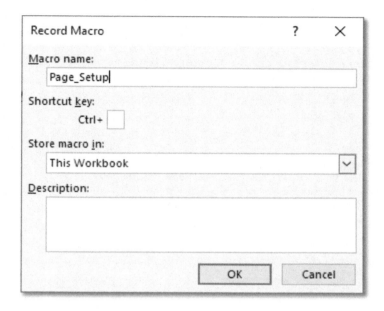

9. Under **Macro Name,** enter **Page_Setup**

10. Click **OK**

11. On the **Page Layout** tab, select **Margins** and choose **Custom Margins**

12. Set the margins to 3cm

13. Click on the **Page** tab

14. Change the **Page Orientation** to **Landscape**

15. Under the **Scaling** label, select **Fit To 1 Page Wide By 1 Tall**

16. Click **OK**

17. Select cells A3:H20

18. On the **Home** tab, in the **Cells** group, select **Format** and choose **Format Cells**

19. Change the **Currency** to **£ English (United Kingdom)**

20. Click **OK**

21. Select the cell range A3:H20

22. On the **Home** tab, format the table styles as **White, Table Style Light 1**

23. Display the **Page Layout** tab, locate the **Page Setup** group, and select **Print Titles**

24. On the **Header/Footer** tab, choose **Custom Header**

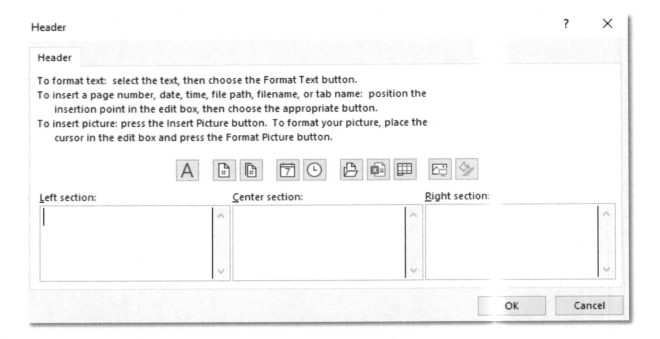

25. In the **Centre Section** area, **Insert File Path**

26. Click **OK**

27. On the **Header/Footer** tab, select **Custom Footer**

28. In the **Centre Section** area, select **Insert Date**

29. Click **OK** and click **OK** again

30. On the **Developer** tab in the **Code** group, select **Stop Recording**

31. Save the workbook and leave it open

Run a Macro

Once a macro records a sequence of steps, it is prepared to complete the saved tasks. Each step recorded in the macro performs when run.

1. With the workbook still open, move to **sheet2**

2. On the **Developer** tab in the **Code** group, select **Macros**

3. Select the **Page_Setup** macro

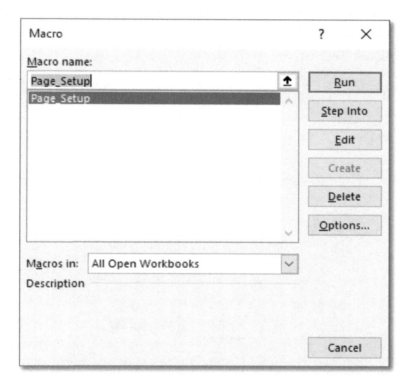

4. Click **Run**

5. The series of commands perform each task, changing the page setup

6. Save the workbook and leave it open

Macro Custom Button

A custom macro button allows you to click on it and run a macro. You click on the macro button, and the sequence of tasks automatically performs each recorded step.

1. With the workbook open, to the right of the **Quick Access Toolbar,** select **Customise Quick Access Toolbar**

2. Select **More Commands**

3. Under **Choose Commands From** select **Macros**

4. Select the **Page_Setup** macro

5. Click on **Add**

6. Select **Modify**

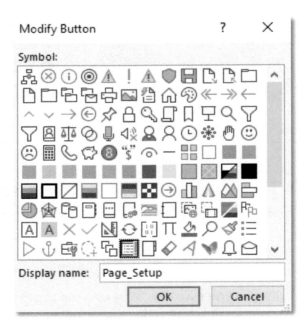

7. Rename the macro as **Page_Setup**

8. Select the **Document** icon for the macro

9. Click **OK** and click **OK** again

10. A button assigns to the **Page_Setup** macro

11. Close the workbook and re-open it

12. Display **sheet3**

13. Click on the button to run the macro

14. Save the workbook as **Macro** and close it

Revision - Section 6

1. Open the workbook **Database function**

2. Select cells D4:D10

3. Apply a name to the cell range called **Age**

4. In cell D11, find the average age using the cell range name

5. Copy the range of cells A3:E10

6. Use **Paste Special** to paste the cells with the same **Values** to Sheet 2

7. Create a **Hyperlink** in cell A1 that links to the website www.digidiscover.com/buy

8. **Edit the Hyperlink** and move it to Sheet 2 cell A1

9. Save the workbook as **Employee Details**

10. Create a new worksheet

11. **Import the Text File Employees** into the worksheet

12. **Record a Macro** that formats the entire table A1:D5 **Orange Table Style Medium 3**, change the font of cells to **Arial** and name it **Format**

13. Create a **Custom Button** with an exclamation mark for the macro

14. Save the workbook

Summary

Excel Productivity

In this section, you have learned how to:

- Apply names to groups of labelled information and formulas

- Use paste special features such as copying values, adding, & subtracting

- Create, modify, and run automated macros

Section 7

Collaborative Editing

In this section, you will learn:

- Share workbooks with other users

- Compare and merge workbooks

- Show and hide formulas in worksheets

Compare and Merge Spreadsheets

You can share workbooks with other users to change information in a workbook copy. The workbook copies merge with the original user deciding what changes to accept or ignore. This helpful feature in Excel allows you to revise and edit workbooks while collaborating with others.

1. Open the workbook **Product Inventory**

2. To the right of the **Quick Access Toolbar,** select **Customize Quick Access Toolbar**

3. Select **More Commands**

4. Under **Choose Commands From** select **All Tabs**

5. Select **Compare and Merge Worksheets**

6. Select the **Add** button to include it on the **Quick Access Toolbar**

7. Select **Customize Ribbon**

8. Under **Choose Commands From** select **All Commands**

9. Create a new group and name it **Changes**

10. Click on the **Add** button to include **Share Workbook (Legacy), Protect Sharing (Legacy)** and **Track Changes (Legacy)**

11. Click **OK**

12. Adjust the colour format of the table range A3:D20

13. On the **Review** tab, select **Share Workbook (Legacy)**

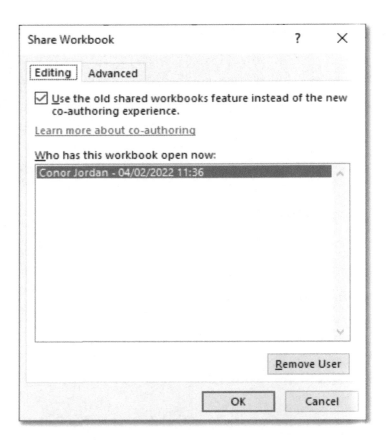

14. Select the **Use the old shared workbooks feature instead of the new co-authoring experience**

15. Click **OK**

16. The workbook is now available to share

17. On the **Review** tab, select **Track Changes (Legacy)** and choose **Highlight Changes**

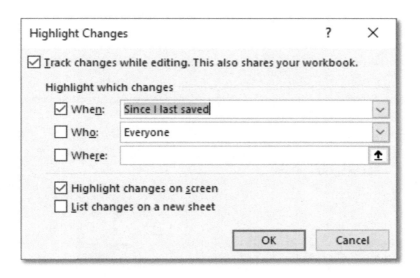

18. Accept the default settings and click **OK**

19. Save the workbook as **Shared**

20. Close the workbook and open it again, acting as another user of the workbook

21. Change the title of the table to **Product Inventory**

22. Name the worksheet tab **Products**

23. Change the value in C7 to 449

24. Change the value in C10 to 49.99

25. Change the value of C16 to 149.99

26. Save it as **Reviewed**

27. On the **Review** tab in the **Changes** group, select **Protect Shared Workbook**

28. Select the **Sharing with track changes** checkbox

29. Enter in a password of **Protect**

30. Click **OK**

31. The shared workbook is now password protected

32. Save the workbook

33. Act as another use of the workbook

34. Select **Track Changes** and choose **Accept/Reject Changes**

35. Click **OK**

36. Accept the first two changes and reject the third and fourth

37. Click **OK**

38. On the **Review** tab, select **Share Workbook (Legacy)**

39. Deselect the **Use the old shared workbooks feature instead of the new co-authoring experience** checkbox

40. Click **OK** and click **OK** again

41. In the **Protect** group, click on **Unshare Workbook**

42. The workbook is no longer shared

43. On the **Review** tab in the **Changes** group, select **Unprotect Shared Workbook (legacy)**

44. The shared workbook is no longer protected

45. Save the workbook

Password Protection

Passwords apply to spreadsheets to protect their contents from other users. The security feature in Excel allows only those who know the password to open protected worksheets. Passwords can then be modified or removed according to requirements.

1.   Open the **Staff List** workbook

2.   On the **Review** tab in the **Protect** group, select **Protect Sheet**

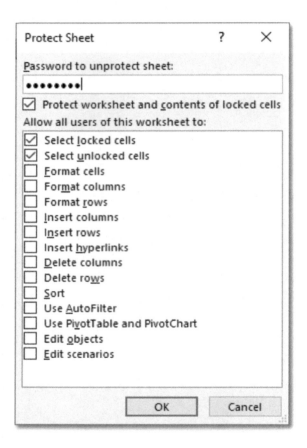

3.   In the **Password to Unprotect Sheet** textbox, type **Password**

4.   Re-enter the password when prompted

5.   Passwords are case-sensitive so ensure that capital and lowercase letters remain the same when entering passwords

6.   Click **OK**

7.   On the **Review** tab in the **Protect** group, select **Protect Workbook**

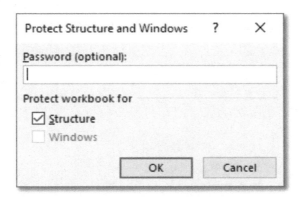

8.   Enter in a password of **Password** and click **OK**

9.   Re-enter the password and click **OK**

10.   Save the workbook and close it

11.   Open the workbook again

12.   Try to delete the table

13.   Deletion is not allowed as the workbook is protected

14.   On the **Review** tab in the **Protect** group, select **Unprotect Sheet**

15.   Enter the password and click **OK**

16.   On the **Review** tab in the **Protect** group, select **Protect Workbook**

17.   Enter the password and click **OK**

18.   The workbook is now unprotected

19.   Save the workbook and leave it open

Password to Open

1. On the **File** tab, click on **Save As,** then select **Browse**

2. Click on **Tools** then **General Options**

3. Under the **File Sharing** label, enter **Open** in the **Password To Open** text box

4. In the **Password To Modify** text box enter **Open**

5. Select the **Read-Only Recommended** checkbox

6. Click **OK**

7. Save the workbook and close it

8. Re-open the workbook

9. Enter the **Open** password to open the workbook

10. Enter the **Open** password to modify the workbook

11. On the **File** tab, click on **Save As,** then select **Browse**

12. Click on **Tools** then **General Options**

13. Delete both passwords and click **OK**

14. There are no longer passwords to open the workbook or modify the workbook's contents. Save the workbook.

Protect Cells

Cell protection prevents other users from changing essential data in a spreadsheet. It helps when collaborating with other users. You can protect cells in a worksheet, allowing only specific cells to be changed, leaving other cells to remain unchanged.

1. Open the **Staff List** workbook

2. Select the range F3:F16

3. On the **Home** tab in the **Cells** group, click on **Format**

4. Select **Lock Cell**

5. On the **Home** tab in the **Cells** group, click on **Format**

6. Select **Protect Sheet**

7. Enter a **Password to Unprotect Sheet** of **Locked**

8. Click **OK**

9. Re-enter the password and click **OK**

10. Try to delete one of the cells from the range F3:F16

11. Deletion is not allowed

12. On the **Home** tab in the **Cells** group, click on **Format**

13. Select **Unprotect Sheet**

14. Enter the password of **Locked**

15. Click **OK**

16. Try to change one of the cells from the range F3:F16

17. It is now allowed

18. Save the workbook and close it

Show/Hide Formulas

Excel allows you to show or hide formulas. This feature checks errors made in formulas.

1. Open the **Logical Functions** workbook

2. On the **Formulas** tab in the **Formula Auditing** group, select **Show Formulas**

3. Notice the formulas displayed in the cell range D4:D6

4. Click on the **Show Formulas** button again to hide the formulas

5. Save the workbook and close it

Revision - Section 7

1. Open the workbook **Sales Figures**

2. **Share the workbook** and make it available to another user

3. Change the title of **Sales Figures** to **Annual Sales**

4. Save the workbook as **Changes**

5. Change B7 to 12000, B9 15000 & B11 to 14000

6. Save the workbook

7. Accept the first two changes to the workbook and reject the third and fourth change

8. Close the **Changes** workbook

9. **Compare and Merge** both workbooks

10. **Accept All Changes** while reviewing the workbook

11. **Apply a Password** of **Secret** to the workbook to **Open and Modify** it

12. Save the workbook

13. **Unshare** the workbook

14. Apply a setting that will not let cells C4:C15 be changed

15. Save the workbook as **Completed**

Summary

Collaborative Editing

In this section, you have learned how to:

- Share workbooks with other users

- Review and edit worksheet information with others

- Applying security features such as password protection to cells, worksheets, and workbooks

Index

Printed in Great Britain
by Amazon

35276246R00093